内蒙古包头博物馆馆藏文物集萃

SELECTION OF BAOTOU MUSEUM COLLECTION

内蒙古包头博物馆

SELECTION OF BAOTOU MUSEUM COLLECTION

馆藏 文物集萃

内蒙古包头博物馆 编

EDITOR BAOTOU MUSEUM

文物出版社

Cultural Relics Press

目　录

CONTENTS

序 一

　　素有塞外明珠、草原钢城美称的包头，地处祖国北疆、内蒙古自治区西部，拥有富庶的河套平原、雄奇的阴山山脉和广袤的达茂草原。中华民族的母亲河——黄河，自西向东流经包头南界，为包头提供了便捷的水上运输。独特的地理位置和多样的自然环境，成就了包头特有的地缘经济模式和丰富多彩的文化特质。

　　自古以来，包头就是农耕经济与畜牧经济相交汇的前沿地带。在几千年漫长的历史长河中，代表农耕经济的中原文明和代表游牧经济的草原文明在这里碰撞交融并相互吸收，最终形成了包头地区既有黄河本色又有草原气息的多元文化特色。

　　早在岁月久远的原始时期，以阿善、西园为代表的新石器时代遗址中，出土了大量的陶器、农业工具、渔猎工具和草原上独有的细石器工具，反映出包头早期先民的生产生活状态，以及蕴涵其中的既有农耕元素、又有草原信息的文化本质。

　　战国秦汉时期，是包头历史上第一个经济发展和文化繁荣时期。随着环境的变迁和统治势力的消长，包头地区先后出现了中原政权和草原政权交替控制，农耕文明与草原文明相互影响的格局。两种文化不断吸收对方的优秀成分，最终形成了博采众长、兼容并蓄，带有地方特色的多元文化。从多姿多彩的岩画，到精美绝伦的文物；从绵延千里、气势恢弘的秦汉长城，到意义深远、古朴浑厚的"单于和亲"瓦当；无不彰显着这一时期包头地区农牧经济同步发展、中原文化与草原文化相融共生的地域特色。

　　元、明、清时期，是包头地区经济文化发展的又一个重要时期。包头地处阴山南北、黄河岸边，是连接东西、沟通南北的通衢要塞，占有得天独厚的地利优势。独特的地理位置和优越的自然环境，成就了包头宜农、宜牧、宜商的经济模式，奠定了包头近代城市形成与发展的基础。

　　随着农牧业经济的进一步发展，各种特色产品迅速增加，中原与草原的商贸活动日益火热。在贸易交往的过程中，也潜移默化地促进了文化的交流和宗教的传播，并最终促成了一个具有水陆码头性质的贸易集散地——包头商埠的形成。

　　以燕家梁元代遗址征集的元青花瓷罐、敖伦苏木出土的元代景教墓顶石、美岱召城门石匾、包头市内征集的清代唐卡等文物为代表，反映了元明清时期包头地区经济、文化发展和各种宗教的传播，见证了各民族相容共生、共同发展，携手创造了开放包容、丰富多元的包头文化的历史。

在包头博物馆同仁的努力下，《内蒙古包头博物馆馆藏文物集萃》终于成书出版，可喜可贺。书中收录的历史文物71件、唐卡38幅、岩画51幅，大多数为包头地区历年来发掘出土文物，以及在本市境内征集的藏品。从一个侧面反映了包头先民为生存而奋斗，是包头先民的创业史、奋斗史，也是包头经济文化发展、各民族交流融合的历史见证。我们在欣赏精美文物的同时，赞赏着古人的严谨认真、精工细做，惊叹于他们的奇思妙想、独具匠心，从中感悟到他们在创作时的从容和淡定。他们是在用自己的双手，创造着自己多彩的生活和梦想的家园，正是这种朴实的精神，成就了今天我们所见到的流光溢彩的文物和博大精深的文化。

在本书出版之际，我对为本书出版付出努力的各位表示敬意，对关心、支持本书出版的有关人士表示衷心的感谢，对包头博物馆事业的发展甚感欣慰。

中共包头市委常委、宣传部部长
2012年9月9日

PREFACE I

Baotou City, known as the Prairie Pearl, the Steel City on Grassland, is located in the western part of Inner Mongolia Autonomous Region, and enjoys the rich Hetao Plain, magnificent Yinshan Mountain and vast Darhan Maomingan Joint League Grassland. The Yellow River, the mother river of the Chinese nation, flows through Baotou from west to east, providing convenient water transportation for the city. The unique geographical position and varied natural environment enable the geopolitical economic model and the colorful cultural characteristics of Baotou.

Since the ancient times, Baotou city has been the front strip of farming and animal husbandry economy. The civilization of Central Plains, representing by farming economy, and the civilization of Grassland, by nomadic economy, collided, blended and learned from each other which finally realized the pluralistic culture feature in this area.

In rude times, a large number of pottery, agricultural tools, fishing and hunting tools and microlithic tools which were broadly and only used in grassland were unearthed from the Neolithic sites such as Ashan and Xiyuan. The production and living condition of the primitive pioneers in Baotou area combines farming elements with nomadic information.

The first period of economic development and cultural boom in Baotou history is from the Warring States Period to Qin and Han Dynasty. Along with the changes of environments and the ruling powers, Baotou was controlled by regimes of Central Plains and Grassland alternatively. A new pattern of farming civilization and grassland civilization influencing each other took shape in this period. Two different cultures absorb from, take the best of and incorporate each other's quality ingredients, and finally form a pluralistic culture with local characteristics. The colorful rock paintings, elegant cultural relics, stretching miles of the Great Wall of Qin and Han Dynasty, and simple and unsophisticated tile-end with inscription of *Marriage of the King of the Huns* (单于和亲) reveal without exception the regional characteristic of the synchronous development of agriculture and animal husbandry economies and the harmonious coexistence of the Central Plains and Grassland cultures.

The period of Yuan, Ming and Qing Dynasties is another important age in the history of economic and cultural development of Baotou area. Located in the north and south of Yinshan Mountain and the bank of Yellow River, serving as a communication connection of the west and east, Baotou city enjoys a richly endowed geographical position and favorable natural environment, which accomplished the economic model of fitting for farming, livestock husbandry and commerce and laid a foundation for the form and development of the modern Baotou city.

With the further development of farming and livestock husbandry and the rapid increasing of all kinds of special products, the commercial activities between the central plains and the grassland conducted in full swing. In the process of trade, cultural exchange and religious spread undertook subtly, finally leading to the formation of Baotou as a commercial port with the feature of land and sea terminals.

Cultural relics such as the blue-and-white jar collected from Site of Yanjialiang, Nestorism Christian tomb stone unearthed from Aolun Sumu City of Yuan Dynasty, stone tablet from Meidai Monastery and Thangka of Qing Dynasty collected from Baotou City concentrate and witness the economic development, cultural exchange and religious spread of Baotou in Yuan, Ming and Qing periods. Different ethic groups coexist harmoniously and develop side by side, creating an open, inclusive and multicultural Baotou.

Under the efforts of the staff of Baotou Museum, we witness the publishing of the catalogue named *Selection of the Baotou Museum Collection*, which is really a fortunate result for those who paid attention to it. All together 71 cultural relics, 38 Thangkas and 51 rock paintings are included in this catalogue, most of which are excavated and collected from Baotou. From one side, this catalogue reflects the history of striving for life of ancient local people, the economic and cultural development and the communication of different ethnic groups in Baotou City. When we enjoy these treasures, we can't resist admiring the delicate, conscientious and keep improving attitude of the craftsmen, praising their intriguing conceptions and creative capability and comprehending their calm and unhurried state in increation. The craftsmen created a colorful life and dream home by their own hands. It is the simple spirit of the craftsmen that enables us to appreciate the splendid cultural relics and the broad culture of our nation.

On the occasion of publishing, I show my respect to all the members who committed to this catalogue, and express my sincere thanks to those who paid attention to it and supported the publication. I really feel comfort to the development of museum career in Baotou City.

Sun Hongmei
Standing Committee and Director of Propaganda Department of
Baotou Municipal Committee of the CPC
September 9, 2012

序　二

　　《内蒙古包头博物馆馆藏文物集萃》即将出版，我代表内蒙古自治区同仁竭诚祝贺。包头博物馆自成立以来，历经十余年努力，已在各方面走在了自治区同行前列。如今，编辑出版此书，更为包头博物馆事业锦上添花。书中所录精品集萃，展示了包头历年来文物成果，再现了包头上下五千年的历史进程。纵览全书，我们可以窥斑知豹，从中了解包头历史的发展脉络，评判历史人物的是非沉浮，畅想包头美好的明天。

　　书中所收内容，可分为三大部分，即包头历史文物、包头藏传佛教唐卡和内蒙古古代岩画。包头历史文物绝大多数为包头历年来发掘出土的文物精品；包头藏传佛教唐卡是包头市文物管理处于1981年在包头废旧物资回收公司征集后移交给包头博物馆的，均属"文革"期间某寺庙遭破坏，唐卡被当作"四旧"物品处理的结果。内蒙古古代岩画来自内蒙古自治区阿拉善盟、巴彦淖尔市和包头市三个区域。

　　馆藏新石器时代文物，以包头东郊阿善、西园遗址出土的文物为代表，包括陶器、石器、骨器、骨石复合工具，以及带有草原特色的细石器，可归为农业生产工具、渔猎工具、狩猎工具、采掘工具、粮食加工工具、炊具、纺线工具、缝制工具、切割刮削工具、乐器、装饰用品等。代表器物有陶质的盆、罐、钵、纺轮、渔网坠、埙等；石质的有铲、斧、锛、刀、砍伐器、球、镞、磨盘、磨棒等。骨质的有针、针筒、簪、锥、鱼钩以及骨石结合的骨柄石刃刀等。

　　上述器物反映了包头史前的自然环境和文化面貌，涵盖了早期先民的生产生活状态、文化渊源以及文化宗教活动。早期先民以原始农业为主，兼营渔猎、采集等辅业。出现了乐器及原始巫术崇拜活动。

　　夏代文物在包头发现很少，馆藏仅有陶质三足瓮，该器物即是生活实用器、又是夏代流行的瓮棺葬的葬具。

　　春秋战国时期文物均为西园春秋墓地出土物，以装饰品为大宗，有少量兵器和生活用品。器形包括骨质与绿松石组成的项饰，青铜动物形饰牌，青铜短刀、镞等，具有明显的北方游牧民族文化特征，属我国北方青铜文化系列。

　　包头博物馆藏汉代文物非常丰富，绝大多数出自包头南郊麻池汉代古城周边的墓葬中，墓葬与古城存在生居死葬的关系，出土器物全面反映了古城的性质与文化状态。文物时代为西汉中期到东汉晚期。包括陶质的壶、罐、案、樽、鼎、灯、豆、奁、盒、井、灶、楼、人物俑、动物俑、方砖、瓦当等；铜质的鼎、钫、壶、熏炉、镜、镞以及铜鎏金弩机等；石质的享堂、墓门等；木质的棺；金质的金箔饰片。

在众多的汉代文物中，最具代表性的是黄釉陶尊，彩绘陶楼，彩绘陶奁，"单于天降"、"单于和亲"瓦当。这些文物基本反映了西汉中期到东汉晚期包头地区的政治、军事、文化和民众的衣食住行。

黄釉陶樽堪称经典之作，它造型古朴浑厚、雍容典雅。尊体外壁雕饰繁缛、层次分明。内容有西王母、神女、玉兔、三足乌、独角羊、翼马、九尾狐、牛首人身、鸡首人身等神怪图案，反映了西汉时期众多的神话故事和普遍流行的黄老思想。

彩绘陶楼、彩绘陶奁反映当时的建筑形式、服装式样，食品烹饪种类和过程。

"单于天降"瓦当反映了南匈奴附汉的历史，"单于和亲"瓦当，印证了汉廷宫女王昭君出塞与匈奴单于通婚和亲的史实。该事件有着重大的政治意义和深远的历史意义，自昭君出塞六十余载，我国北方出现了一派天地广阔、万物自在，经济文化发展、人民安居乐业的繁荣祥和景象。《汉书·匈奴传》形容当时的情形为"三世无犬吠之警，人民无干戈之役"。

北魏时期最典型的文物是固阳县城圐圙古城出土的泥塑彩绘佛像。反映了这一时期佛教在北方地区兴起并广泛传播，也反映了作为北方六镇之一的怀朔镇重要的战略意义。

元明清时期是中国日用品和工艺品制造飞速发展时期，其标志是商品门类大量增加，品种日益丰富，生产工艺日渐成熟，做工精巧细腻、精益求精。各种能工巧匠把制作当成他们的创作舞台，演绎了一个又一个传奇，展示了他们匠心独运、巧夺天工的艺术才华。使中国的传统手艺达到了炉火纯青、登峰造极的辉煌时代。包头博物馆的馆藏文物充分反映了这一历史背景。

元明清文物分瓷器、玉器、铜器、铁器、石雕与石碑、文房、木雕等几大类。精品包括元代青花瓷罐、铁锈花罐、凤鸟形玉冠饰、景教墓顶石、"一捻金"墨，清代粉彩九龙狮耳瓶、素三彩瓷香薰、渠规禁牌石碑、"铭园"贡墨等。这批文物反映了包头地区的经济文化发展历程，是包头由一个商贸集散地向近代城市转型，并最终建埠的历史见证。

以青花罐为代表的燕家梁元代遗址，属当时的蒙汉商贸集散地。该遗址出土了大量内地各窑口的瓷器，主要包括景德镇、钧、定、龙泉、磁州等窑口。元青花罐堪称众多瓷器中的精品，代表了当时的工艺水平和制作典范，是包头博物馆的镇馆之宝。

藏传佛教唐卡，是包头博物馆的一项特色藏品。唐卡为藏语音译，意为绘制在布面上的卷轴画。它具有浓郁的宗教色彩和独特的艺术风格，是藏传佛教传播教义的重要工具，是张挂在寺院殿堂上供信徒尊拜供奉之物，其绘画内容以反映佛教内容的尊像和教义为主。

唐卡的绘制有着严格的规定，画工必须按照佛教经典中的仪轨绘制，从而使唐卡形成了一种独特的绘画方法和程式。在绘画中，采用了中国传统的工笔重彩技法，唐卡绘制所用的颜料均为矿物及植物颜料，并在颜料中添加一定比例的动物胶和牛胆汁，因此，古代唐卡虽经数百年，画面依然色泽艳丽。

包头博物馆藏有唐卡百余幅，多为清代作品，内容包括佛、菩萨、度母、金刚、高僧大德、曼陀罗、佛塔等。这批唐卡基本反映了藏传佛教在包头地区的传播情况，是包头地区藏传佛教最具特色的代表之一。

包头博物馆馆藏岩画是众多藏品中的又一大亮点，所表现的内容是我国北方草原文化发展变化的一个缩影。岩画是一种特殊的文化现象和造型艺术，它以图像的形式记录了北方草原民族为生存而奋斗的连续篇章。由于受自然环境影响，使长期生活在这里的古代先民在社会形态、经济形式、生产方式、生活习惯、审美意识及民族心理等诸多方面都形成了具有草原特色的固定模式，因此，这里保留的岩画，无论是内容还是形式上，都表现出浓厚的草原韵味。

岩画的内容以表现北方草原上常见的羊、马、鹿、虎、豹、狼等动物形象为主。远古时期，北方草原先民与动物的关系最直接、最密切，人们的生活离不开动物，人们的生存依赖于动物，人们或狩猎、或放牧、或祭祀、或娱乐，都反映了人与动物的依存关系。

岩画中有关崇拜内容的图像也占有相当的比例，表现为巫师形象、人面像、太阳神、怪兽、动物蹄印等。

远古时代，由于受到当时社会生产力水平和认知条件的限制，人们对自然界中许多事物及现象都无法做出解释，于是便幼稚地认为，世界上发生的任何事物和现象都受神的支配，即所谓万物有灵、多神崇拜。巫师正是人与诸神沟通的媒介，巫师通过做法，就能将人的愿望上达于神，又能将神的旨意传达于人。这正是岩画中巫师形象普遍流行的重要原因。太阳神崇拜是祈盼太阳神能恩赐人间，阳光普照、风调雨顺。人面像、怪兽图案属部落或部落联盟的图腾标志。动物蹄印属生殖崇拜，祈盼草原牛羊成群、家畜兴旺。

车辆与道路是包头达茂旗岩画中特有的一类内容，说明历史上达茂草原的交通道路十分发达，是内地通向草原的重要通道，从一个侧面印证了学术界推断的历史上存在"北丝绸之路"或"草原丝绸之路"的观点。

包头博物馆馆藏岩画共百余幅，时代从新石器到明清时期，作品多数为凿刻制作，极少数为磨刻或划刻。岩画具有时间跨度长、信息载量大、表现内容丰富、图案制作精美的特点，是包头博物馆不可多得的藏品。

包头博物馆属新建馆，在短短十余年的发展中，能够取得如此骄人的业绩令人敬慕。如今，包头博物馆在各级领导的关心支持下、在社会各界良师益友的鼎力相助下、在各届领导班子和全体同仁的共同努力下，已初步建成了内蒙古自治区颇具特色的博物馆，我为包头博物馆所取得的成绩感到骄傲，对他们的创业精神深感敬佩。

内蒙古博物院院长

2012年9月10日

PREFACE II

On behalf of all my fellow colleagues in Inner Mongolia Autonomous Region, I'd like to congratulate to the publishing of *Selection of the Baotou Museum Collection*, which will make what is good still better after more than one decade's development since the foundation of Baotou Museum. All the selections in this catalogue fully present the archaeological work of Baotou City in the past and represent the historical process of more than 5000 years. I believe the readers of this catalogue will know clearly the developing track of Baotou, judge the historic person objectively and give their imagination free rein while thinking about the future of Baotou.

Three parts can be divided in this catalogue, i.e. historic relics which mainly including the cultural relics excavated from Baotou, Thangkas of Tibetan Buddhism which were destroyed as *Four Olds* (四旧) items with temples during the Cultural Revolution and delivered to Baotou Museum by the Administration of Cultural Relics of Baotou City from the Waste Material Recycling Company in 1981 and ancient rock paintings from Alxa, Bayan Nur areas and Baotou City.

The Neolithic relics, being represented by those from Ashan and Xiyuan sites in the eastern suburb of Baotou, include pottery, stones, bones, bone and stone tools and microlithic tools for farming, hunting, fishing, digging, food producing, cooking, sewing, weaving, cutting, scraping, entertaining, decoration and so on. The representative wares are potteries such as basin, jar, bowl, spindle wheel, fishnet pendant and *Xun* (an ancient egg-shaped, holed wind instrument), stones such as spade, axe, adze, knife, chopper, ball, arrowhead, millstone and roller, bones such as needle, pin canister, hairpin, awl and fishhook and bone and stone tools such as the stone blade with bone handle. These wares reflect the natural environment and prehistoric culture appearance of Baotou, cover the lifestyle, cultural origins and religious activities of the ancestors, show evidences for the economic mode of farming mainly, fishing and hunting and gathering secondarily, the emergence of musical instrument and primitive wiccan activities.

Limited quantity of cultural relics of Xia Dynasty has been found in Baotou. The only one is a pottery three-legged urn which is not only a utilitarian but also tomb furniture for urn burial which was very prevailed in Xia Dynasty.

All the cultural relics of Spring and Autumn and Warring States Periods were excavated from Xiyuan Tomb with ornaments mostly and weapons and daily necessities partly. Ornaments made of bone and turquoise, bronze animal-shaped plaques, gladlii and arrowheads can be easily and commonly found in this tomb. With typical characteristics of nomadic cultures, archaeologists classify them to the series of Northern Bronze Culture.

Baotou Museum enjoys a large collection of Han Dynasty, most of which were from the tombs

016

around Machi City located in the southern suburb, reflecting the feature and cultural classification of the city. The age of the cultural relics ranges from Western Han to Eastern Han, including potteries such as pot, jar, table, cups, *ding* (three-legged tripod or four-legged cauldron), light, *dou* (hemispherical bowl with high stem and spreading foot), *lian* (case for toilet set), bowl, well, stove, building, terracotta, animal figure, squire brick, tile-end and so on, bronzes such as *ding*, *fang*(rectangular pot for holding wine), incense burner, mirror, cross-bow trigger, arrowhead and so on, stones such sacrifice-offering palace, tomb chamber entrance and so on, wood coffins and gold ornaments.

Among all the collection of Han Dynasty, pottery *zun* (cup for drinking) in yellow glaze, painted pottery building and lian, and tile-ends with characters meaning *Endowed Power by the Heaven* （单于天降） *and Marriage of the King of the Huns* （单于和亲） are the mostly representative ones, according to which we can have a clear impression of the politics, military affairs, culture and the basic necessities of local life from Western Han to late Eastern Han in Baotou area.

With its simple, graceful and elegant appearance and complicated arrangement of the ornaments on the surface, Pottery *zun* in yellow glaze can be rated as a classic production. The contents of Queen Mother of the West, fairy, Jade Rabbit, three foot bird, unicorn sheep, Pegasus, Kyuubi Kitsune, beast with cow-head or cock-head and human-body and so on reflect the prevailing of fairy tales and Taoism. Painted pottery building and *lian* represent the architecture technique, clothing style, cooking method and product of that time.

The first tile-end mention above embodies the history of southern Huns' allegiance to the Han regime, while the second, Wang Zhaojun, a Han girl, married the king of the Huns and went abroad to the grassland area, which enjoys an important political and broadly historical significance. In more than 60 years after Zhaojun's marriage, a scene of flouring economy and culture, harmonious society and freely communication emerged in the northern area which was described in *History of Han Dynasty* (汉书) as "*no alarm of barking for three generations, no wars happen among peoples*" （三世无犬吠之警，人民无干戈之役）.

The typical cultural relics of Northern Wei is a painted clay figure of Buddha excavated from Kuluan ancient city in Guyang County, mirroring the rising and spreading of Buddhism and the significant and strategic role of Huaishuo County as one of the top six counties in northern area.

The technique of production of daily necessities and handicrafts advanced rapidly in Yuan, Ming and Qing periods, marking by the increasing of goods categories, the varieties with each passing day, the matured production process, and the improving exquisite craftsmanship. Using production as a platform, the craftsmen created legends one by one, presented their talent by pushing Chinese traditional handicraft to the perfect level and a new era. We can know more about the historical background from the collection of Baotou Museum.

The cultural relics of Yuan, Ming and Qing periods include porcelain, jade, bronze, iron, stone carving, tablet, four treasures of the study and woodcarving. Blue-and-white jar, iron rust jar with flower, jade ornament of crown in phoenix shape, tomb stone of Nestorism and a twist of gold ink of Yuan Dynasty and mixed glaze vase with design of nine dragons and lion-shaped handle, porcelain burner painted in contending colors, tribute ink ingots and so on of Qing Dynasty are among the master pieces. These pieces witnessed the process of economic and cultural development in Baotou area and the transformation from a business distributing center to firstly a rudiment and finally a mature modern city.

The Yanjialiang Site with the representative relics of blue-and-white jar was once a business distributing center in Yuan Dynasty. Porcelains of different kilns such *Jingdezhen, Junyao, Dingyao, Longquan and Cizhou* were also unearthed form the site, among which the blue-and-white jar is a master piece, reflecting the workmanship and being pointed out as a production model and also being the most voluble treasure of Baotou Museum.

Another distinguish feature of Baotou Museum is the collection of thangkas, scroll drawing painted on canvas, of Tibetan Buddhism. With rich religious content such as Buddha and unique artistic style, thangka is an important tool to spread doctrine, which is hanging in temple palaces for believers to worship.

We can see a thangka with bright color even after hundreds years because of the strict process and unique method of drawing. On the base of traditional meticulous re-color technique, the painters use mineral and plant pigments as raw material and add a proportion of animal glue and ox bile.

Baotou Museum enjoys a collection of more than 100 thangkas, most of which are product of Qing Dynasty, reflecting the wide spread of Buddhism. The figures in thangkas include Buddha, Bodhisattva, Tara, Vajra, senior monk, mandala, and pagoda.

Another lights pot is the collection of rock-paintings which minimize the developing process of grassland culture. Rock-paintings record the surviving history of ancient northern nationalities by pictures. Due to the impact of natural environment, the ancient people have their own model of social form, economic form, production methods, living habits, aesthetic consciousness and the national psychology, which also with nomadic characteristics. That is the reason why the rock paintings in this area, whether keep content or form, demonstrates strong grassland flavor.

The common contents of the rock paintings in the northern grasslands are mainly sheep, horses, deer, tiger, leopard, wolf and so on. In the ancient times, northern grassland ancestors had the most direct and close relationship with animals and couldn't live without them. In the activities such as hunting, grazing, sacrifice or entertainment, we can easily find the image of animals, reflecting the interdependence between human beings and animals. A considerable proportion of images related to sacrifice such as wizard, the sun god, Moai statues, monster, animal hoof print and so on also can be found in the rock paintings.

In ancient times, due to the low level of social productive forces and cognitive limitations, people were not able to explain many things and phenomena on the nature, so they naively believed that any phenomena happened in the world are dominated by gods, known as the Animism and Polytheism. In their theory, wizard is exactly the communication medium between human beings and the gods, wizards can convey thoughts and wills of and between them, and that is why wizards are so easily to be seen in rock paintings. The sun god worship is a way to pray for a sunny world and good crop weather, Moai statue and monster are totem signs of tribe or tribal alliance, animal hoof print is a kind of the reproduction worship, praying for gods to bless the prosperity of livestock herds on grassland.

Vehicles and road can only be found in the rock paintings of Damao Banner where is an important channel connecting the grassland and central plains, identifying the developed traffic in this area. From one side, the rock paintings testify the existence of Northern Silk Road or Silk Road on Grassland deduced by the academic circles.

There are more than 100 pieces of rock paintings in Baotou Museum, spanning from Neolithic Age to Ming and Qing periods. Most of the rock paintings are picked and little of them are polished and engraved. The collection enjoy the long time span, big information capacity, rich content and fine design which enable the high value of them.

As a newly-built museum, in ten years' development, under the concern from leaders at all levels, the strong support from friends in social circles and by the leadership and the joint efforts of all colleagues, Baotou Museum has made such a great achievement that my fellow colleagues admire them sincerely. I deeply admire their pioneering spirit.

 Ta La, Director of Inner Mongolia Museum

September 10, 2012

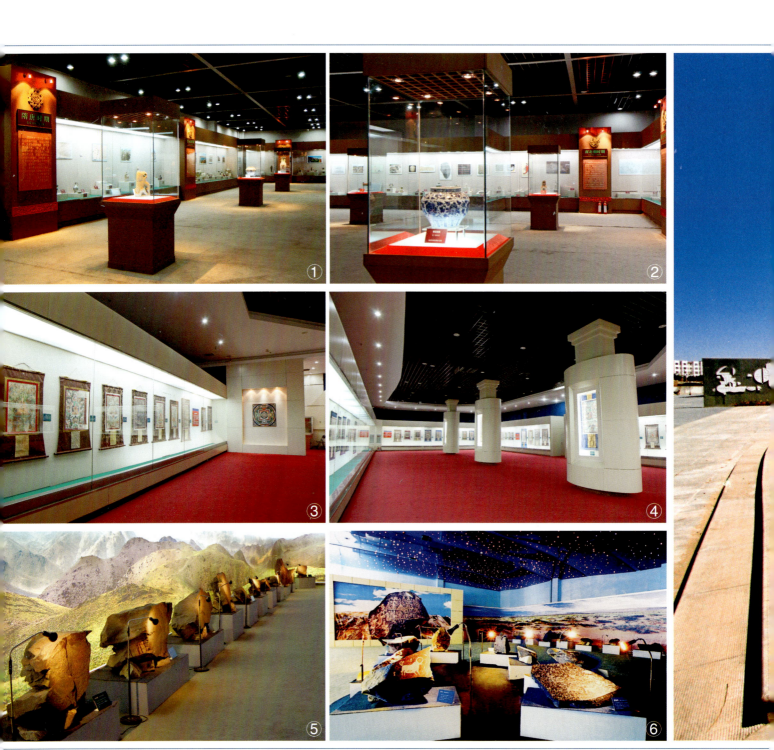

展厅内景   Indoor Scene of Baotou Museum

① ② 历史文物展厅   ① ② Historical Relics Hall

③ ④ 唐卡展厅   ③ ④ Thangka Hall

⑤ ⑥ 岩画展厅   ⑤ ⑥ Rock Paintings Hall

内蒙古包头博物馆外景　于忠诚　摄

Outdoor Scene of Baotou Museum *(by Yu Zhongcheng)*

概　述

内蒙古包头博物馆成立于1998年12月，是一座立足于包头、文物展品涵盖内蒙古西部地区的综合性博物馆。为公益性全额事业单位，正县级规格，在编人员48人，大专以上学历占到90%，其中业务人员占70%，行政人员占30%，拥有高级职称11人，单位内设七个职能部门，业务科室四个、行政科室三个。包头博物馆现有藏品十余万件(套)，经鉴定的三级以上文物165件套。2009年被定为国家二级博物馆。

内蒙古包头博物馆成立之始，就以打造精品陈列为目标，其陈列和展览以精心的策划、精美的设计、精细的制作，赢得了广大观众的一致赞赏和博物馆界专家的广泛好评。2000年，基本陈列被内蒙古自治区文化厅评为"全区50年十大陈列展览精品"，《内蒙古古代岩画陈列》被国家文物局评为1999年度"全国十大陈列展览精品"，《稀土馆》被中国稀土协会评为1999年度全国稀土行业十件大事。

内蒙古包头博物馆新馆于2007年7月27日全面落成开馆，以独具特色的博物馆形象展现在世人面前，向庆祝内蒙古自治区成立60周年献上了厚礼。

内蒙古包头博物馆新馆位于包头市阿尔丁大街友谊广场东南侧，占地3.5公顷，建筑面积2.4万平方米，展厅面积1.5万平方米。与包头美术馆融为一体，展区为三层建筑，一层为美术馆，二、三层为博物馆。她以"草原上的巨石，巨石上的文化"为主题，造型恢宏、内涵深邃。整个建筑宛若巉岩峭拔的山崖，壁立峥嵘，情趣盎然，与友谊广场上的草坪、鲜花、绿树、喷泉相映成趣，构成了既深含文化底蕴，又极具现代韵律的壮美景观，象征着草原文明、黄河文明交相辉映、融会贯通，更似一本展开的历史画卷，给人以遐想。新馆的陈列设计本着突出精品、突出特色，坚持"以人为本"的原则，努力实现思想性与艺术性、科学性与观赏性、教育性与趣味性的完美结合，最大限度地满足不同层次、不同观众群体的审美需求。

内蒙古包头博物馆共设八个展厅，其中六个展厅为常设展厅，展出本馆的基本陈列和专题陈列，另两个展厅为机动展厅，供接待临时展览之用。基本陈列有《包头历史文物陈列》、《内蒙古古代岩画陈列》、《藏传佛教唐卡艺术陈列》、《包头古代石刻文物陈列》；专题陈列有《包头燕家梁元代遗址成果展》、《走向和谐——包头辉煌六十年大型图片展览》。

《包头历史文物陈列》以民族团结、祖国统一和文明进步为主题，荟萃了包头三十年来的考古成就和科研成果，再现了包头地区从新石器时期至清代六千多年的历史。展品中，包头地区出土的新石器时期的陶埙、汉代黄釉陶樽、元代青花瓷罐均为国宝级文物，弥足珍贵。

《内蒙古古代岩画陈列》是包头博物馆最具特色的专题陈列之一，被人们称作是"草原历史的回响"。该陈列系统地展示了内蒙古中西部地区新石器时期至元代的岩画精品。陈列本着"天人合一、回归自然"的设计理念，将岩画生成地达茂草原、阴山山脉、巴丹吉林沙漠的原生态景观通过艺术手段移植到展厅，将新石器时期至元代的岩画精品置于其间，给人以身临其境的艺术感受。

《藏传佛教唐卡艺术陈列》是我国目前唯一的古代唐卡专题陈列。展出的唐卡均为清代至民国时期包头地区藏传佛教的艺术珍品，是中华民族艺术宝库中的绚丽奇葩，在世界艺术史上享有重要地位。该陈列推出后，备受国内外观众的欢迎。

《包头古代石刻文物陈列》是新辟的专题陈列，展出了馆藏的部分石雕、石刻、石碑和石构件等汉、元、明、清时期包头地区生产生活、建筑、墓葬等多种石质文物。

《包头燕家梁元代遗址考古成果展》是内蒙古自治区、包头市两级文物工作者2006年考古发掘的重大成果展览。燕家梁元代遗址位于包头南郊麻池镇境内，是元代内蒙古西部地区的重镇。2006年，内蒙古自治区文物考古研究所和包头市文物管理处为配合工程建设，对遗址进行了抢救性发掘，出土了大量元代景德镇窑、钧窑、定窑、龙泉窑、磁州窑生产的瓷器精品和陶器、玉器、铜器、铁器、骨器、钱币等文物五千余件。该展展出了大量精美的出土文物，使广大观众大饱眼福。

《走向和谐——包头辉煌六十年大型图片展览》是包头市委、市政府为庆祝内蒙古自治区成立60周年举办的大型图片展览。该展以明快的手法、恢弘的效果，通过大量图片，图文并茂地全面反映了内蒙古自治区成立60年来包头市在社会发展、经济建设、文化建设等各个方面所取得的伟大成就。

内蒙古包头博物馆始终遵循"请进来、走出去"的开放式办馆方针，自1999年开始，先后引进了《辽代陈国公主墓出土文物展》、《辽代耶律羽之墓出土文物展》、《辽代壁画展》、《秦始皇兵马俑展》、《圆明园兽首国宝回归展》、《至尊国礼展》、《清代皇室瓷器展》、《草原拾珍——蒙古民族文物展》等几十项精品展。展览期间，博物馆再现了门庭若市、车水马龙的热烈场面。

由内蒙古包头博物馆组织的《草原古韵、塞外风情——内蒙古包头博物馆馆藏岩画、唐卡、文物精品展》先后赴大连、福州、温州、宁波、杭州、广州、武汉、荆州、桂林、柳州、南宁、楚雄等地的博物馆展出，展览历时七年，跨越全国六省区二十多个城市，产生了巨大的社会影响。

内蒙古包头博物馆在学术研究方面硕果累累，先后出版十余部专著，在省级以上专业刊物上发表论文七十余篇，完成国家级研究课题一项，市级研究课题两项，获省级优秀成果二等奖一项，三等奖五项。在内蒙古自治区文博界名列前茅。

包头市是我国北疆的重要城市，有着悠久的历史和灿烂的文化。建设内蒙古包头博物馆，宣传和展示包头及周边地区久远博大的历史文化，展现其灿若星河的奇珍异宝，是一件光荣而又艰巨的任务。内蒙古包头博物馆正以团结进取、求真务实、锐意创新的"包博"精神，着力打造一支高素质的专业团队和具有北方边塞特色的文化品牌，并愿与各兄弟馆联手共建、资源共享，促进交流与合作。充分发挥资源优势，扩大影响，最大限度地创造社会效益和经济效益，为发展文博事业、构建和谐社会做出应尽的贡献。

OVERVIEW

The Baotou Museum, founded in December 1998, is a comprehensive museum based on the culture of Baotou and with exhibits covering the western area of Inner Mongolia Autonomous Region. The Museum is a public welfare institution at the county level with a staff of 48, among which 11 have senior professional title, 90% are with college degree or above, 70% are researchers, and 30% are administrative personnel. There are 7 functional departments, that is, 4 business departments and 3 administrative departments, in the museum. The Baotou Museum enjoys a collection of more than 100 thousands pieces, among which there are 165 pieces at and above level 3. In 2009, the Baotou Museum was identified as national level 2 museum.

Since the beginning of establishment, the Baotou Museum targets at the high-quality goods on display. The careful planning, elegant design and fine production of display and exhibition won the consistent admiration from general visitors and widely praise from experts. The museum has gained honors since its establishment, such as the top 10 displays among Inner Mongolia by the Cultural Bureau of Inner Mongolia Autonomous Region in 2000, the top 10 displays among the nation by the National Bureau of Cultural Relic and the national 10 great things in rare earths industry by Rare Earth Association of China in 1999.

With its unique characteristic, the new Baotou Museum was completed and opened on July 27, 2007, presenting a lavish gift for the 60 anniversary of the Inner Mongolia Autonomous Region.

The new Baotou Museum is located in the south of Friendship Squire in Aerding Street and fused together with Baotou Art Gallery, covering an area of 3.5 hectares and a building area of 24000 square meters. The museum has an exhibition area of 15 thousands square meters which contains 3 floor: art gallery in the first, museum in the second and third. Taking " a boulder on grassland, a culture of boulder " as the theme, as a stretched historical picture scroll , the building, combing cultural deposits and modern breath, the sculpture, lawn, flowers, trees and fountains in the Friendship Square add radiance and beauty to each other, symbolizing the Grassland Civilization, the Yellow River civilization. The new display design, with its outstanding exhibits and features, adheres to the "people-oriented" principle, makes great efforts to realize the perfect combination of the ideological and artistic, scientific and ornamental, educational and entertaining quality and meets the aesthetic demand of different levels and visitor groups maximally.

There are 8 exhibition halls in Baotou Museum, 6 of which are permanent, including 4 basic displays such as Baotou Historical Relics Display, the Inner Mongolia Ancient Rock-paintings Display, the Tibetan Buddhism Thangka Art Exhibition and the Ancient Stone Relics Display and 2 are about special subjects such as the Cultural Relics from the Yanjialiang Site of Yuan Dynasty and the Picture Exhibition of the Brilliant 60 years of Baotou, and 2 are temporary.

Taking national unity, country reunification and civilization progress as the theme, the Baotou Historical Relics Display assembles the archaeological achievements and scientific research of Baotou in the past 30 years, reproduces the six thousand years of history of Baotou area from the Neolithic Age to Qing Dynasty. Among the exhibits, the pottery *Xun*, a kind of ancient musical instrument, of the Neolithic Age, the yellow-glazed *Zun*, cup for drinking and warming wine, and the blue and white porcelain jar of Yuan Dynasty are very precious and among the national cultural relics.

The Inner Mongolia Ancient Rock-paintings Display, presenting the masterpiece of rock-paintings from Neolithic Age to Yuan Dynasty of the middle-west area of Inner Mongolia, is one of the most unique displays in the Baotou Museum and is called "the echoes of the prairie history". With the design concept of "harmony between man and nature, a return to nature", the display transplants the original ecological landscapes of Damao grassland, Yinshan Mountain and Badain Jaran desert to the exhibition hall through different art means, among which high-quality goods from Neolithic Age to Yuan Dynasty are put, giving a vivid art feeling to the audience.

The Tibetan Buddhism Thangka Art Exhibition is the only ancient thangka project display in China and attracts more and more visitors from the nation and the rest of the world. All the items are art treasures of Tibetan Buddhism from Ming Dynasty to the Republican period, and play an important role in world history.

The Ancient Stone Relics Display is a new special subject display. The exhibits include many kinds of stone wares of production, daily living, architecture and tombs from Han, Yuan, Ming to Qing Dynasty such as stone carvings, sculptures, monuments and ornamental pieces for buildings.

The Cultural Relics from the Yanjialiang Site of Yuan Dynasty is an important archaeological exhibition of excavation achievements which was conducted by the two levels of archaeologists in 2006. The Yanjialiang site is located in Machi County, southern part of Baotou, a key town in the western region of Inner Mongolia in Yuan Dynasty. In order to cater for the project construction, Inner Mongolia Institute of Cultural Relics and Archaeology and Baotou Cultural Relics Administration co-excavated the site in 2006. More than five thousand pieces of objects such as porcelains from *Jingdezhen*（景德镇）kiln、*Jun* Kiln（钧窑）、*Ding* kiln（定窑）、*Longquan* kiln（龙泉窑）、*Cizhou*（磁州）kiln and Potteries, jades, bronzes, irons, bones and coins, which will absolutely glut the audiences' eyes.

Moving toward the Harmony: Picture Exhibition of the Brilliant Sixty Years of Baotou is a large picture achievement exhibition held by Baotou Municipal Committee of the CPC and City Government to celebrate the sixtieth anniversary of the Inner Mongolia Autonomous Region. With its unique method, grand effect and abundant exhibits, this exhibition fully reflects the great achievements of social development, economic and cultural construction and other aspects of Baotou in the past 60 years since the establishment of Inner Mongolia Autonomous Region.

Following the principle of the combination of import and export, the Baotou Museum import dozens of exhibitions such as the Exhibition of Cultural Relics from the Princess of State Chen of Liao Dynasty, the Exhibition of Cultural Relics from the Tomb of Yelu Yuzhi of Liao Dynasty, the Rock-paintings of Liao Dynasty, the Tour Exhibition of Terra-cotta Warriors, the Exhibition of Returned Beast-heads from the Summer Palace, the Country Gift Exhibition, the Royal Porcelain Exhibition of Qing Dynasty and the Mongolia Cultural Relics from the Grassland. During the exhibition, the museum was filled again by thousands of visitors.

The Exhibition named the Collections of Paintings, Thangka and Cultural Relics selected and organized by Baotou Museum has been presented in more than 20 museums in diffierent cities such as Dalian, Fuzhou, Wenzhou, Ningbo, Hangzhou, Guangzhou, Wuhan, Jingzhou, Guilin, Nanning, Liuzhou, Chuxiong and so on across 6 provinces in 7 years, which produced a great social effect.

As far as academic research is concerned, the Baotou Museum is also leading the way in Inner Mongolia Autonomous Region. The museum had published 7 monographs, more than 70 articles in professional journals at or above the provincial level, completed 1 national and 2 municipal research subjects, got 1 second prize and 5 third prizes of provincial excellent achievements.

As an important city in the north, Baotou has a long history and splendid culture. It is glorious and difficult task to construct the Baotou Museum, propaganda and display the long history and culture of Baotou and the surrounding and present the treasures of Baotou.

With its belief of unity, progress, practice and innovation, the Baotou Museum strives to create a high quality team of professionals and the culture brand with special characteristics of northern frontier, willing to build museum, share resources, promote exchange and cooperation between the fellow museums, give full play to the resource advantages, expand the influence, create the maximum of social and economic benefits and make our contribution for the development of the career and the construction of a harmonious society.

图版
PLATE

图版目录

石刻 泥塑

玉　器

杂　项

唐　卡

岩　画

包头市

巴彦淖尔市

阿拉善盟

PLATE CONTENTS

CONTENTS OF HISTORICAL RELICS

内蒙古包头博物馆馆藏文物集萃

SELECTION OF BAOTOU MUSEUM COLLECTION

CONTENTS OF THANGKAS

内蒙古包头博物馆馆藏文物集萃 SELECTION OF BAOTOU MUSEUM COLLECTION

CONTENTS OF ROCK PAINTINGS

本书精选的71件（套）历史文物分为骨器、陶瓷器、青铜器、石刻泥塑、玉器、杂项。

骨器主要集中在新石器时代，属阿善、西园遗址中的出土物品，有针、针筒、骨项饰、簪、鱼钩和骨石结合的骨柄石刃刀。均为生产生活用具和饰品。

陶器主要集中在新石器时代和汉代。新石器时代的彩陶较少，素面陶较多，均为生活用器。汉代陶器是包头博物馆一大特色，其中釉陶和彩陶占很大比例，尤以黄釉陶尊、彩绘陶奁为代表，反映了当时的制陶工艺和艺术创作水平。

瓷器主要是以元代和清代居多，元代瓷器以缠枝牡丹纹青花瓷罐为代表，清代瓷器以粉彩九龙狮耳瓶为代表。多为景德镇窑、钧窑、龙泉窑、磁州窑等窑口上的产品。

青铜器从春秋战国到清代都有收藏，较突出的是汉代青铜器。汉代青铜器器形丰富，工艺精湛，此外，还藏有汉、唐、元代铜镜和北魏、清代铜佛像，反映了包头地区历代经济文化的发展状况和铜器流行款式。

石刻包括各个历史朝代的石雕和碑文，有汉代的石墓门、石享堂，北魏的石镇墓兽，元代的景教墓顶石，清代的石碑等。

玉器以元代凤鸟形玉冠饰为代表，为和田白玉圆雕作品，玉质温润，刀法流畅，雕工细腻。反映了元代玉雕的制作水平和审美趋向。

杂项类有金器以及元代的"一捻金"墨、清代的"圆明园图"贡墨和《快雪堂法帖》。金器主要是汉代金箔饰片，内容为各类草原上常见的动物、飞禽以及怪兽、神鸟、神仙等神话动物，多半反映了汉代流行的神话故事。"一捻金"墨墨质优良、墨色黑润，为元代名墨。"圆明园图"贡墨一套八笏，清嘉庆年制，为近代北京著名金石书画家、藏墨家寿玺旧藏，该墨用料精良，为清代徽墨中的上品。《快雪堂法帖》共五卷，清代拓本，为晋、唐、宋、元书法名家法书拓本。

71 pieces of historical relice such as bone artifacts, ceramics, bronzes, carved stones, clay sculptures, jades and others are included in this catalogue.

The bone wares, mostly focusing on the Neolithic Age, excavated from Ashan and Xiyuan Sites, include life utensils and ornaments such as needle, needle-holder, necklace, hairpin, fishhook and the stone blade with bone handle.

Most of the potteries are from the Neolithic Age and Han Dynasty. The painted potteries in the Neolithic Age are very rare, most of which are baldish and life utensils. One of the most characteristic collections in Baotou Museum is the pottery of Han Dynasty, taking yellow glazed Zun and color painted Lian as examples, which reflect the pottery-made technique and creation level of art at that time.

Most of the collections of porcelains in Baotou Museum are from the Yuan Dynasty and the Qing Dynasty, such as blue-and-white jar with decoration of interlocking flower and polychrome vase with design of nine dragons and lion-shaped handle, and are master pieces from Jindezhen Kiln, Jun Kiln, Longquan Kiln and Cizhou Kiln.

The age of bronze collection is from the Spring and Autumn periods to the Qing Dynasty. The varied shapes and exquisite workmanship of the bronze in Han Dynasty, the impressive mirrors of Han, Tang and Yuan Dynasties and the statues of Buddha in the Western Wei period and the Qing Dynasty embody the development of economy and culture and the popular style of bronze in Baotou area.

历史文物
CONTENTS OF HISTORICAL RELICS

骨器 BONE ARTIFACTS
陶瓷器 CERAMICS
青铜器 BRONZES
石刻 泥塑 CARVED STONES CLAY SCULPTURES
玉器 JADES
杂项 OTHERS

The carved stones include sculpture and inscription from the Neolithic Age to the dynasties followed. The stone of the Neolithic include production tools such as axe, adz, knife, plate, millstone and microlith. The representative sculptures are tomb entrance and sacrificial room of the Han Dynasty, animal-shaped chimera of the Western Wei period, Nestorian tomb stone of the Yuan Dynasty and inscription of the Qing Dynasty.

The representative jade ware is a crown ornaments in phoenix and bird shape which is made of Hetian white jade with full relief technique. With its smooth feel, fluent way of cutting and exquisite relief, this ornament witnesses the carving production level of jade and aesthetic tendency in the Yuan Dynasty.

The images of gold wares, mainly gold ornaments of Han Dynasty, are animals that commonly can be seen in steppe, birds and those from fairy tales such as monsters, birds and supernatural beings, which come from the popular fairy tales of Han Dynasty.

Other cultural relics include ink ingot with inscription of *Yi Nian Jin*(一捻金) whose excellent nature and the smooth black color enable its reputation in the Yuan Dynasty, tribute ink stick with scene of the Old Summer Palace, a master piece of ink stick produced at Huizhou of Anhui Province, made in Emperor Jiaqing Era and collected by Shou Xi, a famous painter from Beijing, and Hall of Fast Snow Specimens of Calligraphy, a book of rubbings from calligraphers of the Jin, Tang, Song, Yuan and Qing Dynasty.

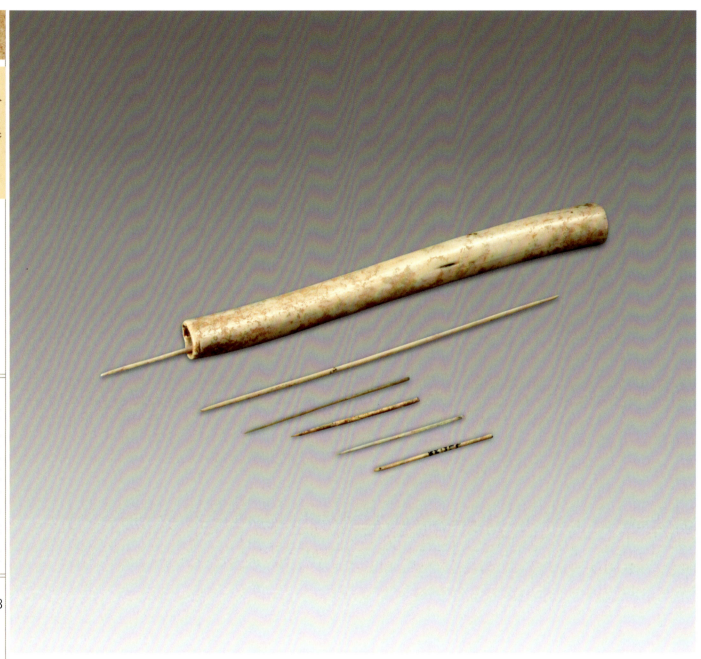

1 骨针、骨针管

新石器时代
针管直径1.54、长15.3厘米，针长3.8~10.5厘米
内蒙古自治区包头市东河区西园遗址出土

Bone needle, needle-holder

Neolithic Age
Diameter of needle-holder: 1.54cm, Length of needle-holder: 15.3cm,
Length of needle: 3.8 ~ 10.5cm

骨针是用动物细骨制成的，分圆和扁两种，针体表面光滑，针尖
锐利，针孔清楚。骨针管是截取动物肢骨一段，再精工磨制成规
整器形。骨针管无纹饰，磨制光滑。

2 骨柄石刃刀

新石器时代
长14.6、宽3.2 厘米
内蒙古自治区包头市东河区阿善遗址出土

Knife with bone handle and stone blade
Neolithic Age
Length: 14.6cm, Width: 3.2cm

刀柄由动物肢骨劈裂成两半作柄体。柄呈长方
形，末端呈扁平状，钻有一孔，一侧开有"V"
形细槽用于镶嵌石片，骨柄无纹饰；石刃由两片
不规整、质地不同的长方形石叶组成，石叶双面
有齿。刀背刻有符号。骨柄石刃刀是新石器时代
出现的小型复合工具。

内蒙古包头博物馆馆藏文物集萃
SELECTION OF BAOTOU MUSEUM COLLECTION

3 骨尖状器

新石器时代
长29.5厘米
内蒙古自治区包头市东河区西园遗址出土

Bone pointed implements
Neolithic Age
Length: 29.5cm

是用动物肢骨劈裂两半做成的，一端尖，另一端较宽，磨光，是
新石器时代的生产或生活用具。

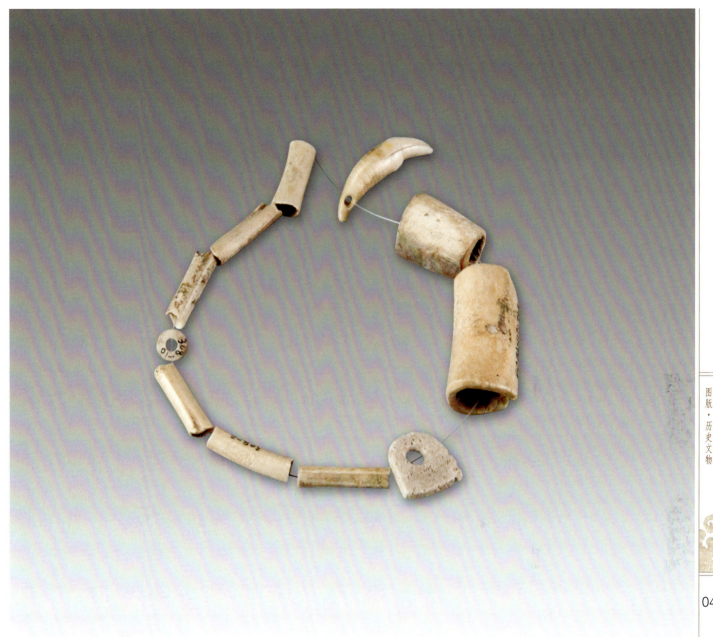

4 **骨项饰**
新石器时代
内蒙古自治区包头市东河区阿善遗址出土

Bone necklace
Neolithic Age

由11块大小不一、磨制光滑的骨管、骨
牙、骨环组成，是古代装饰品。

5 绿松石骨项饰

春秋时期
长29.5厘米
内蒙古自治区包头市东河区西园遗址出土

Bone necklace with turquoise

Spring and Autumn Period
Length: 29.5cm

绿松石骨项饰由268个不规则的骨管和五块绿松石连接而成，绿松
石绿中泛蓝。

6 双孔陶埙

新石器时代
口径2.2、腹径5.2、孔径0.6、高4.6厘米
内蒙古自治区包头市东河区西园遗址出土

Double-holed pottery *Xun*
(an ancient egg-shaped, holed wind instrument)
Neolithic Age
Diameter of mouth: 2.2cm, Diameter of belly: 5.2cm,
Diameter of hole: 0.6cm, Height: 4.6cm

泥质灰陶，呈椭圆形，外观像鸟卵。表面磨光，手制而成。
埙身有一个吹孔，两个发音孔，可以吹奏出五个音符。陶埙
是我国最古老的吹奏乐器之一。

7 折腹陶钵

新石器时代
口径11.4、底径5.8、高12.1厘米
内蒙古自治区包头市东河区阿善遗址出土

Folding-belly pottery bowl

Neolithic Age
Diameter of mouth: 11.4cm, Diameter of bottom: 5.8cm, Height: 12.1cm

泥制灰陶，敛口，深折腹，平底。腹部有三圈连点锥刺纹，下腹部
刻有一女巫形象，女巫双手上举，双腿叉开，做向天祈祷的动作，
反映原始宗教崇拜。

8 网格纹彩陶钵

新石器时代
口径26.4、底径10.8、高11.3厘米
内蒙古自治区包头市东河区西园遗址出土

Painted pottery bowl with quadrilateral net design
Neolithic Age
Diameter of mouth: 26.4cm, Diameter of bottom: 10.8cm,
Height: 11.3cm

泥制红陶，敛口，折腹，平底。口沿部绘菱形网格纹，陶
钵两侧近口沿处有两孔。

9 马家窑双耳彩陶罐
新石器时代
口径10、底径7.5、高16.5厘米
青海省西宁市文化局赠

Double-handled painted pottery jar, Majiayao type
Neolithic Age
Diameter of mouth: 10cm, Diameter of bottom: 7.5cm, Height: 16.5cm

侈口、卷沿、鼓腹、平底，颈部有两耳，施红衣褐彩，口沿内侧饰黑彩菱形纹和锯齿纹，颈部饰黑彩线纹，腹部饰变体蛙纹。

10 马家窑双耳彩陶壶
新石器时代
口径9.7、腹径26.7、底径11、高36.5厘米
青海省西宁市文化局赠

Double-handled painted pottery pot, Majiayao type
Neolithic Age
Diameter of mouth: 9.7cm, Diameter of belly: 26.7cm,
Diameter of bottom: 11cm, Height:36.5cm

侈口、斜颈、鼓腹、平底，下腹部有两桥形耳，表面磨光施褐彩，口沿内侧饰水波纹，颈部饰斜线纹，腹部饰弦纹和变体蛙纹，双耳上方饰人面纹。

11 马家窑双耳彩陶罐

新石器时代
口径10、腹径18.3、底径7.5、高16.3厘米
青海省西宁市文化局捐

Double-handled painted pottery jar, Majiayao type

Neolithic Age
Diameter of mouth: 10cm, Diameter of belly: 18.3cm,
Diameter of bottom: 7.5cm, Height: 16.3cm

侈口、溜肩、鼓腹、平底，颈部有两耳，施褐彩，
口沿内饰波浪纹，颈部饰竖波浪纹，肩部、腹部饰
弦纹、连珠纹，下腹部饰菱形纹。

12 陶三足瓮

夏
高57.5、口径26厘米
内蒙古自治区包头市昆都仑区征集

Three-legged urn

Xia Dynasty
Height: 57.5cm, Diameter of mouth: 26cm

泥质灰陶，器壁较薄，器口略呈椭圆形，方唇，敛口。
近口沿处磨光，卵形腹，圜底。底部有三个小乳状袋
足，瓮身饰细绳纹。器身有一道裂纹，裂纹上有两两相
对的四个修补孔，整体保存完好。

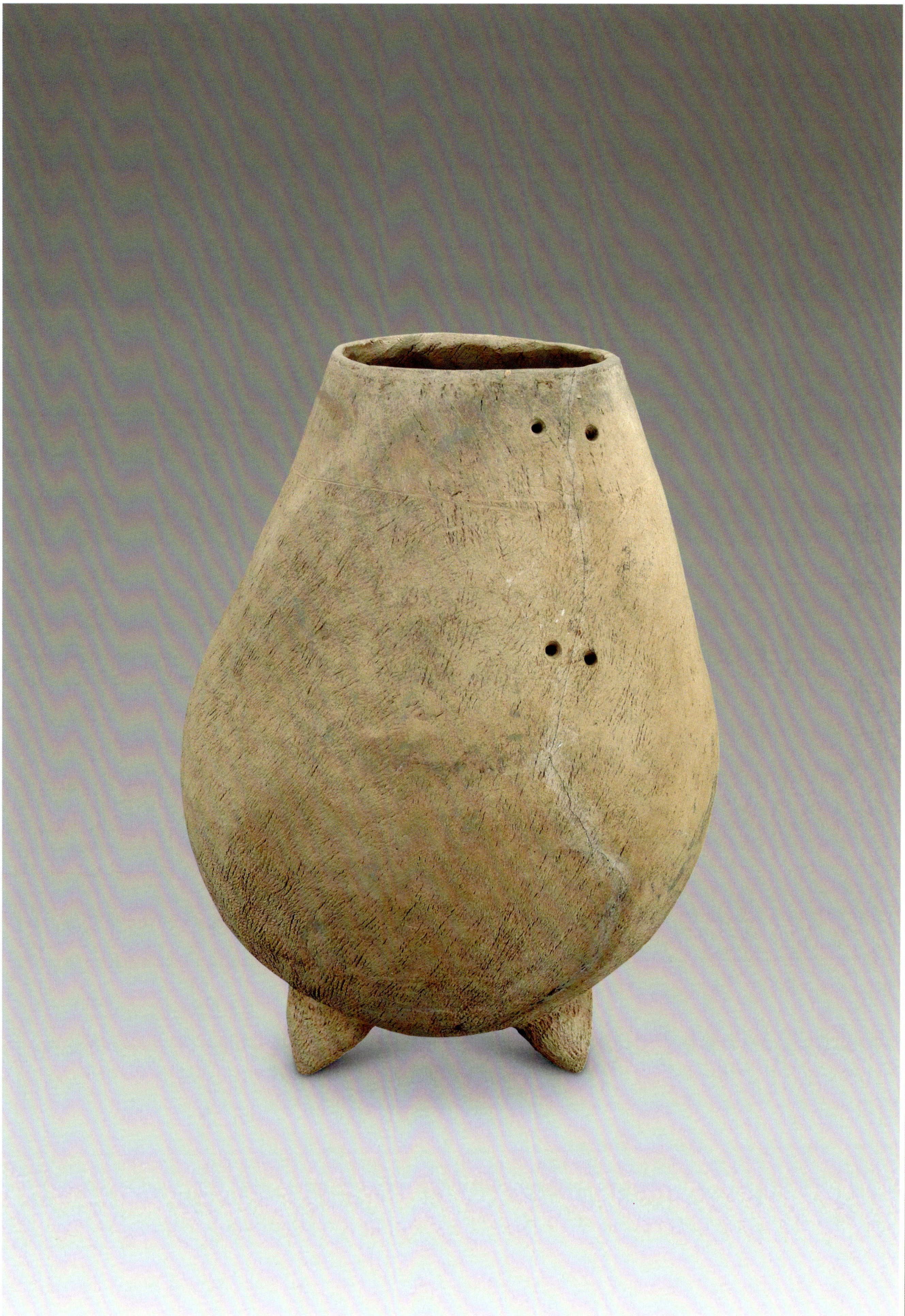

13 "千秋万岁" 瓦当

汉

直径17.7厘米

Tile-end with inscription of *Qian Qiu Wan Sui*
（千秋万岁）, an auspicious saying
Han Dynasty
Diameter: 17.7cm

瓦当被十字均分四格，十字中心有一大乳突覆盖十字面，十字边轮为变体卷云纹。"千秋万岁"四字为篆书。

14 "单于天降"瓦当

汉
直径17.1、筒长28厘米
内蒙古自治区包头市九原区召湾47号汉墓出土

Tile-end with inscription of _Endowed Power by the Heaven_ (单于天降)
Han Dynasty
Diameter:17.1cm, Length of the tile: 28cm

瓦当面为圆形,为四分式,铭文"单于天降"篆书分别写于四分式之中,"十"字棱线整齐。瓦当边轮较宽。瓦筒施绳纹,筒上有一直径近2厘米的圆孔。属记事文字瓦当,"单于天降"文字反映出西汉中晚期匈奴呼韩邪单于归附汉廷的历史事件。

15 "四夷尽服"瓦当

汉

直径18厘米

内蒙古自治区包头市九原区召湾47号汉墓出土

Tile-end with inscription of *the King of All the Minorities* （四夷尽服）

Han Dynasty

Diameter: 18cm

瓦当面为圆形，为四分式，铭文"四夷尽服"篆书分别写于四分式之中，"十"字棱线整齐。瓦当边轮较宽。瓦筒施绳纹。瓦当属记事文字瓦当，反映出西汉中晚期匈奴呼韩邪单于附汉及天下安定的历史事件。

16 "单于和亲"瓦当

汉

直径15.5厘米

内蒙古自治区包头市九原区汉墓出土

Tile-end with inscription of *Marriage of the King of the Huns* （单于和亲）

Han Dynasty

Diameter: 15.5cm

瓦当面为四分式，"十"字单线，边轮较宽。年代当为西汉晚期，与历史上昭君出塞事件有关。

17 "富乐未央 子孙益昌"方砖
汉
长32.5、宽32、厚度5.7厘米
内蒙古自治区包头市九原区召湾91号汉墓出土

Brick with inscription of *Pray for Never Ended Rich and Happy Life and Prosperous Later Generations*（富乐未央 子孙益昌）
Han Dynasty
Length: 32.5cm, Width: 32cm, Thickness: 5.7cm

呈方形，系实心砖，正面印有阳文篆书"富乐未央 子孙益昌"两行八字，文字的两侧用菱形纹作装饰。

18 黄釉陶樽

汉

口径18.7、腹径21.3、通高22.1、足高3.7厘米

内蒙古自治区包头市九原区召湾47号汉墓出土

Yellow glaze pottery Zun (cup for drinking or warming up wine)
Han Dynasty
Diameter of mouth: 18.7cm，Diameter of belly: 21.3cm，Height: 22.1cm，
Height of leg: 3.7cm

樽为筒状，子母口，口径略大于底径，壁微斜，蹲熊式三足。变体博山式盖，盖有两条曲折弦纹，近口沿处和底部有一周山峦，腹部布满浮雕图案，内容有上古神话、瑞禽怪兽、甲胄武士、舞蹈戏乐等六组图案，图案清晰，光泽莹润，是汉代流行的纹饰图案。

19 四神陶博山炉

汉
口径7.2、底径9、高18厘米
内蒙古自治区包头市九原区召湾86号汉墓出土

Pottery Boshan incense burner with four supernatural beings
Han Dynasty
Diameter of mouth: 7.2cm, Diameter of bottom: 9cm, Height: 18cm

由炉盖、炉身、底座三部分组成。炉身似豆形，博山式盖，炉身和底座连成一体。炉盖上镂空浮雕四神，即青龙、白虎、朱雀、玄武，底座盘中有一龟负起博山炉体。在挺拔峻峭的山峦间，青龙张着大口，身躯健硕，气宇轩昂；白虎瞠目张口，威武雄健；朱雀口衔宝珠，昂首翘尾，威严鸷猛；玄武为龟蛇合体，蛇弯曲盘绕着龟身，龟仰首爬向山顶，这种布局错落有致，紧凑而不呆滞，沉稳中又显活跃。

20 黄釉陶灶

汉
长22.3、宽18.2、高16.3厘米
内蒙古自治区包头市九原区汉墓出土

Yellow glazed pottery oven
Han Dynasty
Length: 22.3cm, Width: 18.2cm, Height: 16.3cm

圆形，灶面五眼，灶台略鼓，灶头稍钝，五釜眼上各置一釜，有
圆形烟囱孔，灶门呈长方形，两侧有挡风。

21 彩绘仕女纹陶方奁

汉

长41.2、宽27.6、高12.5厘米

内蒙古自治区包头市九原区张龙圪旦汉墓出土

Painted pottery _Lian_ (a cylindrical covered vessel used as a cosmetic box) with classical ladies

Han Dynasty

Length: 41.2cm, Width: 27.6cm, Height: 12.5cm

奁为长方形，方唇，宽平沿，四角及侧边带小方足，足绘红彩，器底有一椭圆形孔。奁正面用红彩绘边框，框内彩绘五个汉代妇女，均侧身跪坐，身体略前倾，双手前拱。

22 彩绘陶楼

汉

最宽49.2、最厚27.7、高53.5厘米

内蒙古自治区包头市九原区张龙圪旦汉墓出土

Painted pottery building

Han Dynasty

Width at most: 49.2cm, Thickness at most: 27.7cm, Height: 53.5cm

楼平面呈长方形，楼顶为四阿式，上有一斗三升两铺作，三面坡，前面两垂脊各饰瓦当，后面两垂脊作挡墙式，前顶饰瓦棱纹，前檐均有瓦当，瓦当饰点状纹，侧顶有浅瓦棱纹无瓦当，楼门为长方形，楼侧墙壁有两椭圆形孔，楼后墙残，楼绘红、白两彩。

23 褐釉剔刻花瓷罐

西夏
口径18.9、腹径35、底径15.3、通高38厘米
内蒙古自治区包头市征集

Brown glazed porcelain jar with cut decoration

Western Xia
Diameter of mouth: 18.9cm, Diameter of belly: 35cm, Diameter of bottom: 15.3cm,
Height: 38cm

胎制坚硬，胎体厚重。在口沿下饰有藤条堆塑。整个器物施褐釉，上腹部以两组剔划牡丹纹为主体图案，图案上下各刻两道弦纹，整体造型端庄大方，纹饰流畅精细。

24 青花缠枝牡丹纹瓷罐

元
口径20.5、腹径34.5、底径19.3、高28.1厘米
内蒙古自治区包头市九原区麻池镇燕家梁征集

Blue-and-white jar with design of interlocking peony
Yuan Dynasty
Diameter of mouth: 20.5cm, Diameter of belly: 34.5cm,
Diameter of bottom: 19.3cm, Height: 28.1cm

在淡蓝匀润的釉色上，分段饰以花卉图案，颈部绘花草纹，肩部
饰石榴花卉，腹部为富丽的缠枝牡丹，下腹部饰卷草纹和变形仰
莲纹，各组图案之间以两道弦纹为界，层次分明，构图完美。

25 磁州窑白釉褐花盖罐

元

口径16.2、腹径29、底径12.3、高36.3厘米

内蒙古自治区包头市固阳县公益民乡红涯湾捐赠

White glazed brown covered jar, *Cizhou* Kiln

Yuan Dynasty

Diameter of mouth: 16.2cm, Diameter of belly: 29cm,

Diameter of bottom: 12.3cm, Height: 36.3cm

盖为子母口塔形顶，盖边缘略上翘，盖上饰点状纹和弦纹，器身肩部饰点状纹，腹部以草叶纹隔"花"字。下腹部饰一周水波纹。各组图案之间均用两周弦纹相隔。

26 磁州窑白釉褐花四系罐

元
口径4.4、腹径18.6、底径9.3、高28.4厘米
内蒙古自治区包头市东河区征集

White glazed brown jar with four rings, *Cizhou* Kiln
Yuan Dynasty
Diameter of mouth: 4.4cm, Diameter of belly: 18.6cm, Diameter of bottom: 9.3cm, Height: 28.4cm

肩颈间附贴四系，器身通体施白釉，以褐色花纹装饰，肩部饰点状纹，腹部饰涡纹草叶纹。

27 磁州窑孔雀蓝釉黑彩花草纹盖罐

元

口径8.2、腹径15.6、底径7.4、高18厘米

内蒙古自治区包头市达尔罕茂明安联合旗额尔登敖包墓葬出土

Peacock blue covered jar in black color with floral decorations, *Cizhou* **Kiln**

Yuan Dynasty

Diameter of mouth: 8.2cm, Diameter of belly: 15.6cm, Diameter of bottom: 7.4cm, Height: 18cm

通体施孔雀蓝釉，在蓝釉中饰黑彩纹饰，近底部无釉。带盖，盖上饰草叶纹。器身用弦纹间隔成三部分，肩部为卷云纹，腹部为花草纹。

28 钧窑天青釉碗

元
口径14.7、底径5.54、高7.4厘米
内蒙古自治区包头市九原区元代燕家梁遗址出土

Sky blue glazed bowl, *Junyao* Kiln
Yuan Dynasty
Diameter of mouth: 14.7cm, Diameter of bottom: 5.5cm, Height: 7.4cm

天蓝釉，外壁挂半釉，圈足内外无釉，釉面多鬃眼，有紫斑。

29 蓝釉白花棒槌瓶
清
口径9、腹径11、底径8.5、高29厘米
内蒙古自治区包头市东河区征集

Blue glazed bottle with white floral design in wooden club shape
Qing Dynasty
Diameter of mouth: 9cm, Diameter of belly: 11cm,
Diameter of bottom: 8.5cm, Height: 29cm

直口，圆唇，直颈，长直腹，平底圈足，施蓝釉，绘白色梅花纹。

30 素三彩瓷熏炉

清

长20、宽19.5、高27.5厘米

内蒙古自治区包头市征集

Simple three colors incense burner

Qing Dynasty

Length: 20cm, Width: 19.5cm, Height: 27.5cm

炉体呈方形，镂空盖，盖顶有狮钮，炉身饰四条黄地绿彩、紫彩螭龙和花卉纹，四兽足。

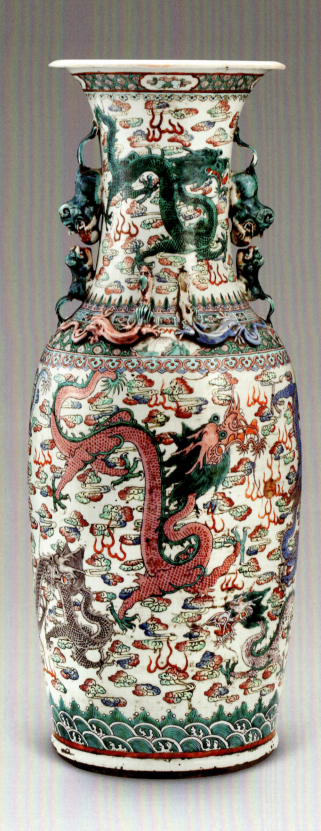

31 双狮耳粉彩瓷瓶

清
口径27.8、腹径32.2、底径27、高79.8厘米
内蒙古自治区包头市征集

Famille rose porcelain bottle with two lion-shaped handles
Qing Dynasty
Diameter of mouth: 27.8cm, Diameter of belly: 32.2cm,
Diameter of bottom: 27cm, Height: 79.8cm

瓶颈部有一对由大小两只狮子组成的狮耳，肩部浮雕四条头尾相对的龙，
颈部、腹部彩绘九条龙和祥云纹、火珠火焰纹，底部绘海水纹，口沿部绘
仙桃纹，口沿内绘花卉。通体施釉，釉色白中微闪灰，底部无款识。龙的
造型生动，属清代晚期典型龙纹样式，龙嘴大张，龙眼鼓突于外，八字形
龙须弯曲外撇，头顶两侧歧分鹿形双角，长披龙发，龙身用鱼鳞纹装饰，
弯曲成弓形，龙爪为四爪；龙的釉色色彩缤纷，有蓝、绿、青、紫、褐、
白、红等色；龙首或昂扬或回顾，龙身或盘曲或舒展，姿态各异。

32 动物形铜佩饰

战国
宽2.7、高3.3厘米
内蒙古自治区包头市九原区西园遗址出土

Animal-shaped bronze ornament
Warring States Period
Width: 2.7cm，Height: 3.3cm

佩饰似虎形，呈站立状，为古代北方民族饰品。

33 双环首青铜短剑

战国
长25.2、宽4.3厘米
内蒙古自治区包头市土默特右旗征集

Double-ring-headed bronze sword
Warring States Period
Height: 25.2cm, Width: 4.3cm

直柄、直刃、双环首、束腰、中脊起棱，柄与剑身衔接
处两侧有突齿，柄身连铸，剑整体瘦长，素面无纹饰。

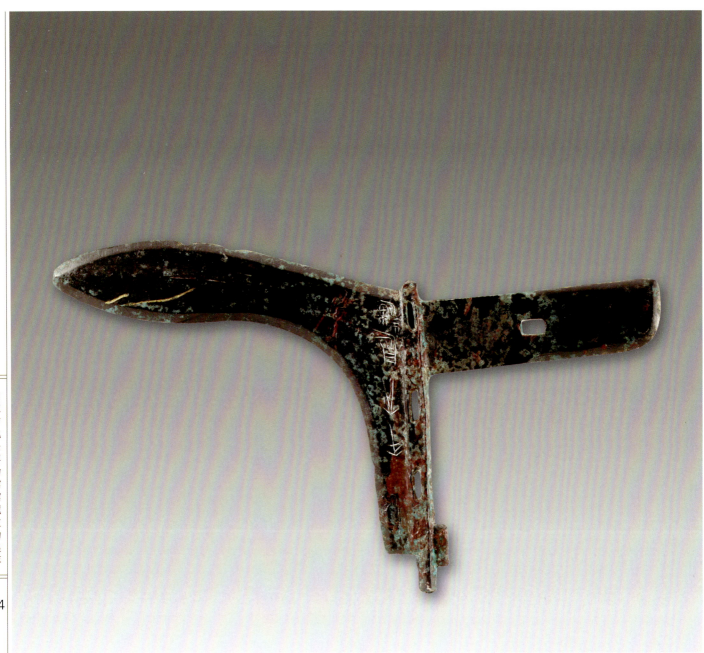

34 青铜戈

战国
长21.7、宽10.8厘米
内蒙古自治区包头市征集

Bronze *Ge* (a dagger-axe)

Warring States Period
Length: 21.7cm, Width: 10.8cm

内刃戈，狭援胡单刺，援后段较前段更狭。戈有铭文。

35 素面铜镜
战国
直径11厘米

Plain bronze mirror
Warring States Period
Diameter: 11cm

素面，桥形钮。

36 铜鎏金弩机
汉
长13.5、宽10.2厘米
内蒙古自治区包头市九原区召湾42号汉墓出土

Gilt bronze *Nu*(cross-bow)
Han Dynasty
Length: 13.5cm, Width: 10.2cm

鎏金，由望山、钩牙、悬刀、枢四部分组成。望山呈长方形，中间有凹槽，钩牙呈三角形。弩机是古人远射兵器弩的一个组成部分，是用于发射弓箭的一种装置。

37 双耳三足铜鼎

汉

口径17.4、腹径23.5、高21.3厘米

内蒙古自治区包头市九原区召湾51号汉墓出土

Bronze *Ding* (tripod for cooking meat and cereals) with two ears and three legs

Han Dynasty

Diameter of mouth: 17.4cm, Diameter of belly: 23.5cm,
Height: 21.3cm

敛口，子母口无盖，上腹部有一对称桥形方耳，耳中间镂空，上部稍向内斜，鼓腹、圆底，蹄形三足，腹部饰一周凸棱。

38 铜钫

汉

口边长10.2、底边长11.8、高36厘米

内蒙古自治区包头市九原区召湾46号汉墓出土

Bronze *Fang* (a rectangular jar)

Han Dynasty

Length of mouth brim: 10.2cm,
Length of foot brim: 11.8cm, Height: 36cm

为方形壶。方口，窄平沿内折，长颈，垂腹，外撇的方形足，腹侧有一对铺首衔环，素面。

39 铜熏炉

汉

口径11、腹径14.6、柄长10.3、通高15.8厘米

内蒙古自治区包头市九原区召湾45号汉墓出土

Bronze incense burner

Han Dynasty

Diameter of mouth: 11cm, Diameter of belly: 14.6cm,

Length of handle: 10.3cm, Height: 15.8cm

盖与炉体为子母口扣合成一球体，盖顶镂空为火焰纹，像一团正在燃烧的
火焰，盖中央为半圆状扁提钮。器身素面、圆腹，在腹部有一周凸棱装
饰，腹部的一侧有细长柄，圆底、蹄形三足。

40 铜灶

汉

长21.2、最宽处15.1、高8.3厘米

内蒙古自治区包头市九原区麻池镇汉墓出土

Bronze oven

Han Dynasty

Length: 21.2cm, Width at most: 15.1cm, Height: 8.3cm

灶面平，头尖，呈船形，置一大二小三釜眼；釜眼上各置一釜，灶前有一小圆形烟囱孔，下有蹄状四足，灶门呈长方形。

42 铜熏炉

汉

口径11.7、底径23.5、高19.5厘米

内蒙古自治区包头市九原区麻池镇汉墓出土

Bronze incense burner

Han Dynasty

Diameter of mouth: 11.7cm, Diameter of bottom: 23.5cm,
Height: 19.5cm

由炉盖、炉体、底盘组成。炉盖与炉体为子母口，盖面纹饰为镂空草叶纹，盖中央为桥形提钮。炉体为圆形，腹部有两周弦棱，细柄、圈足，足部饰草叶纹，圆形底盘，盘底有兽形三足。

41 铜博山炉

汉

口径10.8、底盘直径13.1、高23.1厘米

内蒙古自治区包头市九原区召湾88号汉墓出土

Bronze Boshan incense burner

Han Dynasty

Diameter of mouth: 10.8cm,
Diameter of tray: 13.1cm, Height: 23.1cm

由炉盖和炉体两部分组成。炉盖和炉体之间以子母口相接，炉盖镂空，盖上部为重叠的山峦形，下部有七个孔。炉体鼓腹、实柄，柄上饰两圈竹节状纹，柄座为圆盘、空心，座外圈施流云纹，座外缘有一圈凸棱。

43 昭明铜镜

汉
直径17.8厘米
内蒙古自治区包头市九原区汉墓出土

Bronze mirror with inscription of *Zhao Ming*（昭明）
Han Dynasty
Diameter: 17.8cm

圆形，球形钮，十二连珠纹钮座，镜背有篆体铭文两周，内周为"内清
质以昭明，光辉象夫日月，心忽扬而愿忠，然雍塞而不泄"二十四字。
铭文两侧为突起的宽弦纹。宽弦纹两侧均有栉齿纹，外周铭文为"洁清
（精）白而事君，怨阴雕（欢）之合□使玄锡之流泽志疏，而日忘糜美
之愿□亟可母之□恺外女纪"。素宽缘，缘内有栉齿纹一周。

44 双耳铜釜

北魏
腹径20.5、高26厘米
内蒙古自治区包头市达尔罕茂明安联合旗腮忽洞出土

Double-eared bronze *Fu* (a cauldron)
Northern Wei
Diameter of belly: 20.5cm, Height: 26cm

炊具。口微侈，深腹、高圈足，口沿有两桥形耳，腹部有一周弦纹。

45 铜佛像

北魏
最宽7、高15.3厘米
内蒙古自治区包头市固阳县征集

Bronze Statue of Buddha
Northern Wei
Width at most: 7cm，Height: 15.3cm

佛像高肉髻，眼若纤月，眉细长弯曲，鼻翼丰满，嘴角微翘，棱角分明。长颈削肩，体态修长，身披帔帛，帔帛在肩部呈三角巾形，帔帛在腹部交结并穿过一环，然后上卷搭于手臂。下着长裙，裙下摆呈锯齿状。右手上举作施无畏印，左手下垂作予愿印。跣足而立于圆座，座下有方形柱，缺底座和背光，佛背有两拱形钮，钮上有孔。

46 "延兴三年"铜佛像

北魏
宽8、高14厘米
内蒙古自治区包头市固阳县怀朔镇城圐圙村出土

Bronze Buddha with inscription of *Yan Xing San Nian*（延兴三年）
Northern Wei
Width: 8cm，Height: 14cm

佛面相方圆适中，鼻子修长高挺，薄唇，大耳，发髻纹饰为浅波浪状。身着通肩式大衣，衣纹结构呈U形，线条隆起，衣纹在尾端分两叉如燕尾状。右手作施无畏印，左手作予愿印，跣足而立。底座残。舟形火焰纹背光，火焰纹细瘦，形似夔龙，头后有圆形头光，头光饰莲花纹。佛像背面刻有："延兴三年岁在癸丑正月十五日清信士□□□为亡父母造无量寿佛一区愿令父母聆生之处西方无量寿佛回生一会说口愿在其例。"竖五列共五十三字。

47 环首铁刀
北魏
通长94.3厘米
内蒙古自治区包头市固阳县征集

Chain head knife
Northern Wei
Length: 94.3cm

半圆形环首，刀身较长，刀背直，一面有刃。

48 双凤衔绶纹葵形铜镜

唐
直径27.2、厚0.6厘米
内蒙古自治区包头市金属公司征集

Mallow-shaped bronze mirror with two phoenixes biting a ribbon design
Tang Dynasty
Diameter: 27.2cm, Thickness: 0.6cm

葵花形，圆钮，素沿。镜背分内外两区，内区钮的两侧对称浮雕一对鸾鸟，两只鸾鸟形
状相同，其头部有花冠，曲颈挺胸，展翅翘尾，其尾羽很长且卷曲飘逸；鸾鸟口衔花叶
形双穗长绶带，足踏花枝；钮的上下各雕有莲花，莲花硕大，果实累累，枝蔓婉转。在
外区配有八朵花枝，内外相映成趣。

49 海兽葡萄铜镜

唐
直径11.3、厚0.8厘米
内蒙古自治区包头市征集

Bronze mirror with beasts and grapes design

Tang Dynasty
Diameter: 11.3cm, Thickness: 0.8cm

圆形，兽钮，连珠纹高圈分为内外两区。内区为四只形态各异的瑞兽绕钮奔跑，间以葡萄蔓枝叶实；外区饰飞禽葡萄蔓枝叶实；边缘纹饰为流云纹。

50 仙人龟鹤带柄铜镜

宋
直径9.9、通长18厘米
内蒙古自治区包头市金属公司征集

Bronze mirror with handle and immortal, turtle and crane decorations

Song Dynasty
Diameter: 9.9cm, Length: 18cm

镜面圆形，无钮，镜柄为长方形，窄平素边缘，镜面主题纹饰为神仙龟鹤图。其格局为三分法，上部是明月当空、桂枝环绕，桂树枝条苍劲、疏密有致；中部为茂盛的不老松下端坐着一仙人，仙人束高髻，身着长袍，手拿一拂尘，盘坐于石上，仙人身后有圆形背光，仙人右边立一侍者，侍者的双手持幡，仙人的左边有一只仙鹤展翅翱翔；下部有一神龟延首伸颈、蹒跚爬行。神龟的下面是祥云飘逸，仙鹤、神龟似听到神仙的召唤，正向仙人奔去。

51 "富民县官"铜镜

金

直径17.8、厚0.7厘米

内蒙古自治区包头市征集

Bronze mirror with inscription of *Magistrate who Enriching Local People*（富民县官）

Jin Dynasty

Diameter: 17.8cm, Thickness: 0.7cm

圆形，半球形钮，素宽沿。主题纹饰浮雕一条巨龙，巨龙首尾相对，吞云吐雾，翻卷盘绕，造型刚劲有力。在巨龙的龙身与镜缘间点缀一周缠草卷云纹，镜缘上錾刻"富民县官"四字和一个花押。"富民县官"四字字体纤细清晰，并在镜缘錾刻着官府验记和押记。

52 庑殿式浮雕释迦牟尼铜鎏金佛龛

辽

通高16.2、宽10.6厘米

内蒙古自治区包头市征集

Gilt-bronze niche with a pitched woof for statue of Sakyamuni

Liao Dynasty

Height: 16.2cm, Width: 10.6cm

佛龛造型为长方形，顶为庑殿式。采用浮雕技法，雕刻内容为释迦牟尼居中而坐，面相丰圆饱满，肉髻低矮平缓，螺发正中嵌一髻珠，前额宽阔，两肩宽厚，身躯饱满。衣纹如小蛇般婉曲。有背光，结跏趺坐于束腰仰莲纹座，莲瓣肥硕。周围浮雕有六十二个佛像。佛龛做工精细，浮雕精美。

53 "首领"铜印

西夏
长5.3、宽5.3厘米
内蒙古自治区包头市固阳县征集

Bronze seal with inscription of *Leader* (首领)
Western Xia
Length:5.3cm, Width:5.3cm

圆角方印，印文为西夏文，且上下对称，汉语意为
"首领"，系白文九叠篆文。印文周边圆角加边，
印台较薄，为柱形钮，钮上刻西夏文"上"字，钮
两侧各刻四个西夏文字，左侧刻授印的年款，右
侧刻受印人姓名，钮底部有一小孔，为印绶绾结之
处，印采用翻砂浇铸而成。

55 铁锏
元
长73.5厘米
内蒙古自治区包头市九原区征集

Iron mace
Yuan Dynasty
Length: 73.5cm

长而无刃，四棱。

54 铜火盆
元
口径45、高12.7厘米
内蒙古自治区包头市土默特右旗征集

Bronze brazier
Yuan Dynasty
Diameter of mouth: 45cm, Height: 12.7cm

敞口，平沿，直腹，三兽足。

56 铜鎏金无量寿佛像
明
底座宽14、高19.7厘米
内蒙古自治区包头市九原区征集

Gilt-bronze statue of Anitayus
Ming Dynasty
Width of the bottom: 14cm, Height: 19.7cm

头戴宝冠，梳着高髻，面微低，面相饱满，宽额高鼻薄嘴，嘴角微
翘，眼睑微垂，双眉与鼻胫相连，面含微笑，大耳铛垂肩，上身袒
露，颈戴项圈，胸饰璎珞，臂饰宝钏，肩部圆润，中腰敛收，下着
长裙，裙摆垂于台座上，裙纹繁缛，线条流畅。双手做禅定印，双
手上下叠放在屈盘的双腿上，手捧宝瓶，瓶口生长着一朵吉祥花
卉，结跏趺坐于莲花台座上。佛像的底座束腰内收，座上饰仰覆莲
花纹，莲花瓣上下对称分布，莲花瓣宽肥饱满。佛像全身镶嵌有红
宝石、绿松石，显得雍容华贵。

57 铜鎏金大威德金刚像
清
高12.3厘米
内蒙古自治区包头市征集

Gilt-bronze statue of Yamantaka
Qing Dynasty
Height: 12.3cm

通体鎏金，其造型是常见的九头三十四臂十六足。在九面中的正面为一牛头形状，最上面的一个头是文殊菩萨形象。主尊怀抱明妃罗浪尕娃，其余三十二臂均拿各种法器，十六条腿呈左伸右屈状。明妃是一面两臂，头戴五骷髅冠，长发下垂，左手持碗，右手拿着钺刀，左腿抬起，右腿伸开。二者均赤裸，足下底座缺失。

58 石享堂

汉

长130、宽118、高140厘米

内蒙古自治区包头市九原区召湾98号汉墓出土

Stone hall for worship of ancestors

Han Dynasty

Length: 130cm, Width: 118cm, Height: 140cm

享堂为砂质岩制成，由屋顶、左侧墙、支柱、基座、后墙五部分
组成，无右侧墙和前墙。享堂顶为四阿式顶，四垂脊，正脊两端
雕莲花瓦当，前面两垂脊左边立雕俯卧青龙，右边立雕俯卧白
虎，后面两垂脊两端雕莲花瓦当。享堂顶内中央立雕一莲花纹，
四周浮雕柿蒂纹。享堂顶边缘有凹槽与后墙、左墙凸棱相咬合。
左侧墙平面呈方形，后墙为长方形，墙板内外两面四周边框突
起，上下两角有矩形缺角，以便将上下两边插入顶部。享堂右前
角立一石支柱，支柱上有一圆柱榫插入顶部凹槽，柱头装饰为仰
莲纹饰，柱身浅浮雕盘龙纹饰，柱底为碗形，与基座凹槽咬合，
基座平面为长方形四角修成台阶状，在基座左侧、后方有凹槽与
后墙、侧墙呈榫状咬合。

59 石墓门

汉
单扇宽45、厚9、高116厘米
内蒙古自治区包头市九原区汉墓出土

Stone entrance of the tomb

Han Dynasty
Width of each piece: 45cm, Thickness: 9cm, Height: 116cm

墓门雕刻着精美的辅首衔环、双鱼和朱雀图案。辅首衔环是古代庭院大门上的装饰，也是石刻画像的常见图案。墓门的饕餮辅首，造型夸张，头顶三锐角，口衔环、双鱼，面目狰狞恐怖。墓门上的凤凰形象稍有不同，系一雄一雌，右为雄，称为"凤"；左为雌，称为"凰"。辅首衔环、双鱼和朱雀墓门的规制证明墓主人是一位有地位有德行的人。

61 蟠龙莲花纹石镜座

北魏
直径16.5、厚4.7厘米
内蒙古自治区包头市固阳县城圈圐村出土

Stone mirror stand with lotus and dragon design
Northern Wei
Diameter: 16.5cm, Thickness: 4.7cm

砂质岩制成。镜座中间有一圆形柱洞，上部为鼓状，顶
部雕两条蟠龙，周围雕莲花纹，下部高浮雕三条蟠龙，
雕刻精美。

60 石镇墓兽

北魏
宽19.1、厚21.2、高35.2厘米
内蒙古自治区包头市固阳县怀朔镇城圈圐村征集

Stone beast to ward off evil
Northern Wei
Width: 19.1cm, Thickness: 21.2cm, Height: 35.2cm

灰色砂石岩。圆雕兽面，大眼圆睁，宽鼻阔口，张嘴露齿，面部
狰狞恐怖。四爪有力，前腿柱立，后腿弯曲蹲踞于平板上。宽
胸挺背，昂首向上，颈部悬一铃铛。脊背上有竖直排列的六个乳
凸，周身雕刻皮毛线纹。

62 石碑额

明
宽108、厚20、高80厘米
内蒙古自治区包头市土默特右旗征集

Top part of a tablet
Ming Dynasty
Width: 108cm, Thickness: 20cm，Height: 80cm

蟠龙碑首为双龙戏珠造型，两条粗壮有力的巨龙倒盘在两侧，龙
爪共同抓握一颗宝珠，珠下为略呈长方形的碑额，一面字迹不
清，一面隐约可见篆刻"大千"二字，其下为仰莲纹。

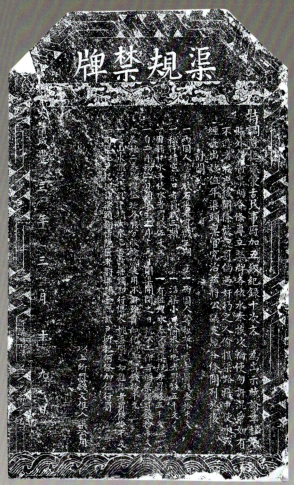

63 渠规禁牌石碑

清

宽49、高78厘米

内蒙古自治区包头市东河区沙尔沁乡西园
村征集

Stone tablet of prohibition

Qing Dynasty

Width: 49cm，Height: 78cm

碑为灰色花岗岩石，碑额楷书"渠规禁牌"
四字，并饰蝙蝠祥云纹。碑首及左右两侧装
饰折带纹，碑下方装饰小波纹。碑文楷书，
上款"特调萨拉齐蒙古民事府加五级纪录十
次文：为出示晓谕章程，张贴外合，将裹明
各条专立禁碑，各依水奉挨次轮使，勿许混
争。如有不遵者，按照后开条款认罚。倘遇
奸巧之人，偷损渠路，暗中使水，或经查
出，该值年渠头裹官究治，兹将公议定规各
条开列于后：计开……"，落款："大清咸
丰三年三月十九日"。

64 彩绘泥塑菩萨头像

北魏

最高13厘米

内蒙古自治区包头市固阳县怀朔镇城圐圙村出土

Painted clay sculpture of Bodhisattva's head

Northern Wei

Height at most: 13cm

戴莲花宝冠，高肉髻，头发在额正中分两组，发际线
略呈尖拱形，面相丰圆端庄，眉毛高挑，眼细长，鼻
梁高隆，嘴角上翘，面带微笑。面敷白粉或红粉。

65 白玉佩饰

元

宽5、高5.2厘米

内蒙古自治区包头市达尔罕茂明安联合旗额尔登敖包墓葬出土

White jade pendant

Yuan Dynasty

Width: 5cm, Height: 5.2cm

镂空，雕花鸟纹，外形呈心形状。

66 凤鸟形玉冠饰

元

长4.7、高2.9、厚1.3厘米

内蒙古自治区包头市固阳县银号大德恒征集

Phoenix- shaped jade crown ornament
Yuan Dynasty
Length: 4.7cm, Height: 2.9cm,
Thickness: 1.3cm

和田青白玉。采用了圆雕与透雕相结合的雕刻手法。凤鸟头戴高冠，小圆坑形鸟眼，鸟嘴宽而长，鸟颈细长，鸟身横托。凤鸟的尾部镂空，长尾分叉外卷，站在有阴刻线的条形玉台上。头部、双翼、底座均阴刻有细线，颈部、尾部和底座连接处镂空。

67 玉帽顶饰

元

宽4、高3.6厘米

内蒙古自治区包头市达尔罕茂明安联合旗额尔登敖包墓葬出土

Jade ornament on top of hat
Yuan Dynasty
Width: 4cm, Height: 3.6cm

白玉，镂空，帽顶饰。

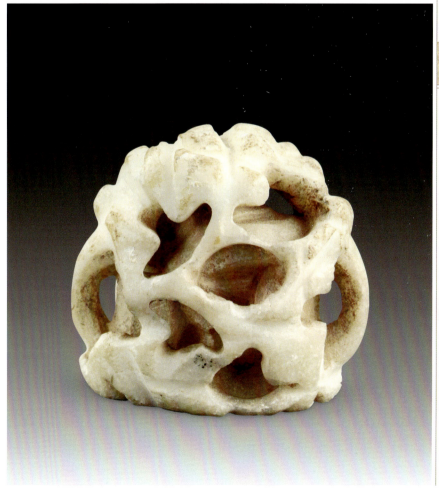

内蒙古包头博物馆馆藏文物集萃
SELECTION OF BAOTOU MUSEUM COLLECTION

69 "一捻金"墨锭

元
直径15.1、厚0.89厘米
内蒙古自治区包头市达尔罕茂明安联合旗额尔登敖包墓葬出土

Ink ingot with inscription of *Yi Nian Jin*（一捻金）
Yuan Dynasty
Diameter: 15.1cm, Thickness: 0.89cm

墨呈圆饼形，用模范压制而成。墨的正面中部印有楷体阳文"一捻金"三字，是墨的名称，墨的背面中部印有竖行"王道宾造"四字，王道宾是制墨的工匠。此墨锭墨质优良，色泽黑润，墨上的字体方润整齐，笔画刚劲有力。"一捻金"墨是元代名墨，是难得的墨中精品。

113

68 动物形金箔片

汉
内蒙古自治区包头市九原区召湾汉墓出土

Animal-shaped gold pieces
Han Dynasty

金箔片原为漆器上的饰件，是古人将金箔剪制成各种造型贴嵌在漆器上，作装饰之用。这批金箔片按其造型可分四类：一是动物类，有龙、虎、鹿、犬、狐、兔、马、牛、羊、骆驼、怪兽、鸵鸟、狮、豹、猫等；二是禽鸟类，有凤凰、孔雀、鹰、雁、鹳雀、神鸟等；三是人物造型，有仙人捉蛇降妖、人面怪兽、羽人等；四是各种生活用具，有壶、罐、瓶等。

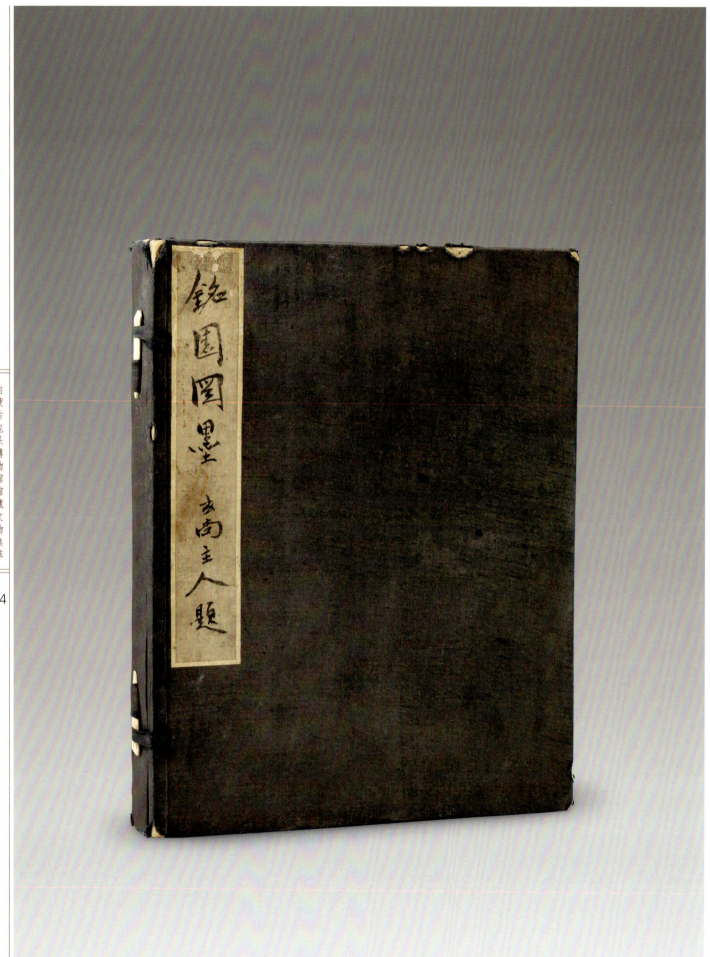

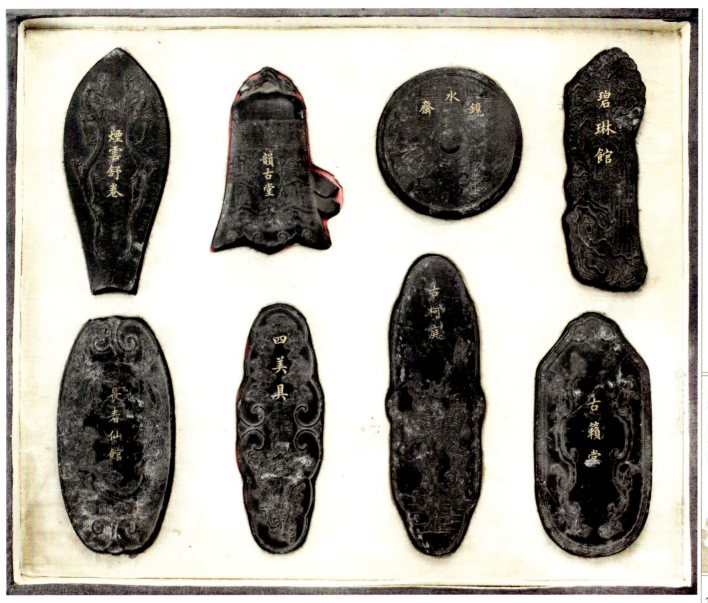

70 "圆明园图" 贡墨锭

清
"烟云舒卷" 宽4.3、高9.7厘米
内蒙古自治区包头市东河区征集

Tribute ink sticks with scene of the Old Summer Palace
Qing Dynasty
Height: 9.7cm, Width: 4.3cm

此墨一套八笏,第一笏随形两面镌绘灵石翠竹,正面楷书"碧琳馆"。第二笏如意圭首、圆脚,正面居中楷书"古籁堂",左右双螭拱卫,背面镌楼阁,阁中陈列琴磬。第三笏铜镜形,正面居中一钮,左右龙飞凤舞,下方瑞兽,水云间以番莲花朵,上方楷书"镜水斋";背镌绘烟波浩渺,岸边屋舍隐现于蕉石丛中。第四笏卷边牛舌形,面镌古木奇石,上方楷书"古柯庭";背镌古木参天,阁中几案上置书卷瓶梅,阁后巨石耸立。第五笏卷边牛舌形,正面下方镌蟠龙,上方云气中楷书"四美具";背上方龙凤翔翥,下方一麒麟,昂首与龙凤呼应。 第六笏莲瓣形,正面左右双龙对舞,中间楷书"烟云舒卷";背镌疏柳清波,水榭亭台掩映其间。 第七笏牛舌形,正面烟云中二螭上下遨游,中部楷书"长春仙馆";背镌崇山峻岭,碧松紫芝生于岩间石上。第八笏钟磬形,正面中部楷书"韵古堂",左侧楷书阳识"臣阮元恭进"名款;背额楷书阳识"嘉庆年制",中镌一狮,左下部二磬凸出,周遭饰以各种花纹并镌古文六字。除第八笏外,其余七笏右侧皆楷书阳识"嘉庆年制"。

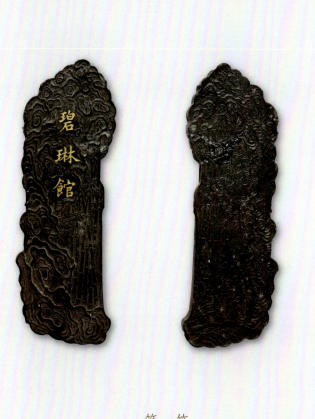

第一笏

第二笏

第三笏

第四笏

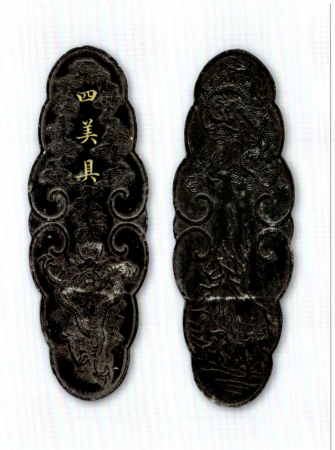

第五笏

第六笏

第七笏

第八笏

71 《快雪堂法帖》卷

清

长34.1、宽18、厚3.9厘米

内蒙古自治区包头市征集

Kuai Xue Tang (Hall of Fast Snow) Calligraphy

Qing Dynast

Length: 34.1cm, Width: 18cm, Thickness: 3.9cm

《快雪堂法帖》五卷，硬木面，有签无题。拓工较佳，
墨色较浓，为改刻后的内拓本。卷首以王羲之《快雪时
晴帖》为冠，故名。所刻晋、唐、宋、元法书，起于王
羲之，迄于赵孟頫，凡二十一家。卷一为王羲之、王献
之及赵孟頫等帖，卷二为王洽、王廙、颜真卿、怀素、
高闲、李建中、柳公权、欧阳询、褚遂良、徐浩等帖，
卷三为宋高宗、苏轼、蔡襄、吴琚、张即之、薛绍彭等
帖，卷四为黄庭坚、米芾、苏轼等帖，卷五为米芾、蔡
襄、赵孟頫等帖。

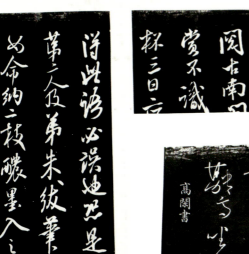
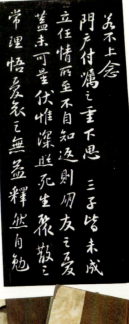

内蒙古包头博物馆馆藏唐卡百余幅，书中选用38幅，均为清代作品。主要表现藏传佛教内容，描绘有各种佛、菩萨、罗汉、度母、佛母、天王、财神、护法诸神、高僧大德、曼陀罗等尊像。从唐卡的分类看，主要以国唐中的彩唐为主。这批唐卡基本反映了藏传佛教在包头地区的传播情况。

Baotou Museum enjoys a collection of more than 100 thangkas, 38 pieces of which are included in this catalogue and are of Qing Dynasty, reflecting the wide spread of Tibetan Buddhism in Baotou area. The figures in thangkas include Buddha, Bodhisattva, Arhat, Tara, Buddha mother, Vaisravana, the god of wealth, legal guardian, senior monk, mandala, etc. From the view of classification, most of the thangkas are color thangkas.

1 佛传图

清
长84.5、宽54.5厘米
内蒙古自治区包头市废旧回收公司征集

Map of Bnddhist enlightenment

Qing Dynasty
Length: 84.5 cm, Width: 54.5 cm

这是一组描绘释迦牟尼佛一生教化事迹唐卡中的其中一幅。释迦牟尼佛一生的重
要事迹有如"四相图",即画佛陀"诞生、成道、说法、涅槃"四件事;"八
相图",画佛陀"受胎、诞生、出游、逾城、降魔、成道、说法、涅槃"八件
事;又如"十二相图"等等。佛传图也称《释迦牟尼百行图》、《释迦牟尼业迹
图》,有一百幅,也有一百零八幅的。在这些画传中描绘了释迦牟尼佛在过去生
中为菩萨时种种教化众生的事迹,称之为本生图。

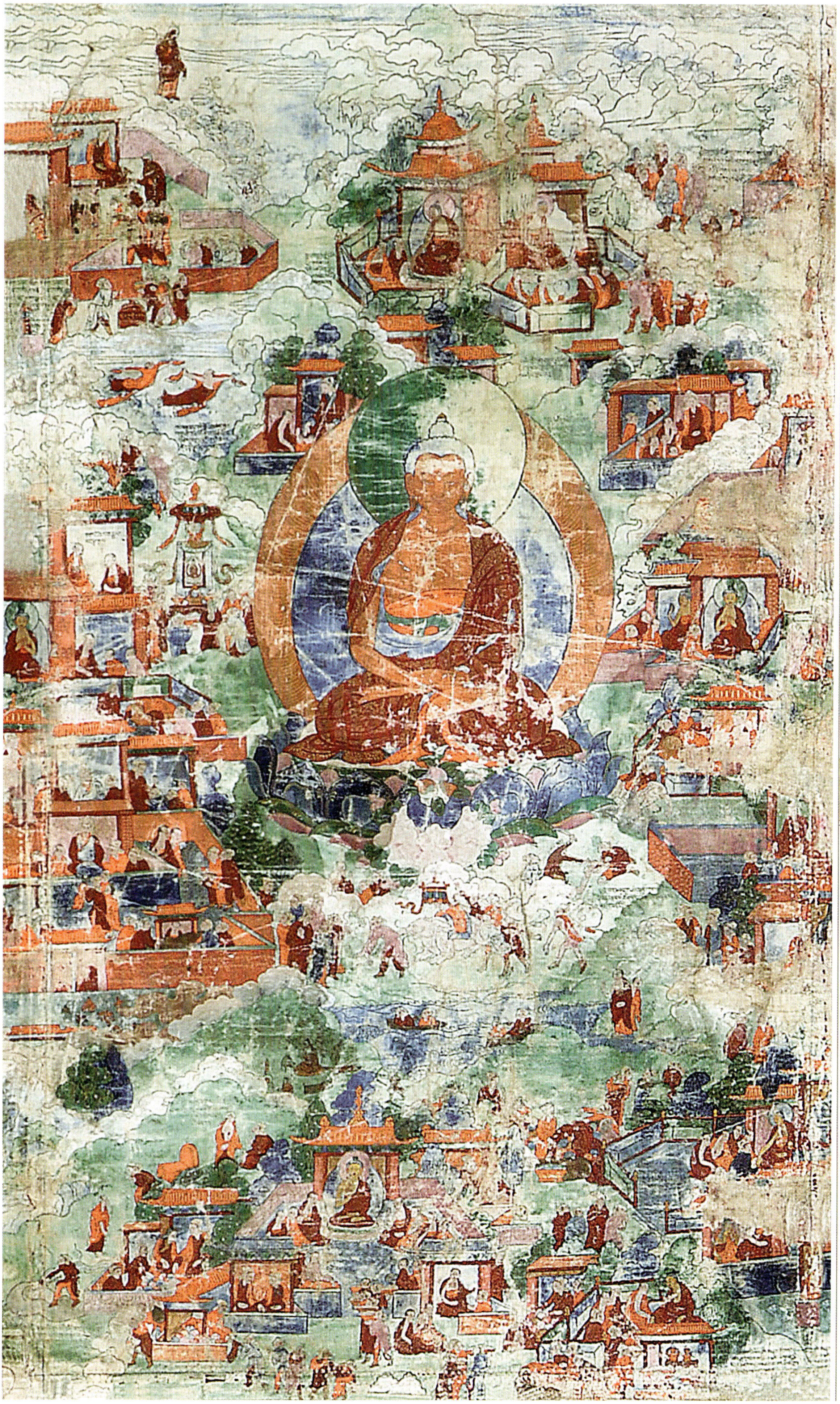

2 佛传图

清
长88、宽55.6厘米
内蒙古自治区包头市废旧回收公司征集

Map of Bnddhist enlightenment
Qing Dynasty
Length: 88 cm, Width: 55.6 cm

本画幅保存较好，画面中部为释迦牟尼，周边绘传教、讲法的宗教内容，还有描绘世俗生活的场景。右上角黑色的帐篷、牦牛、几个牧女在背水或歇息，下方群鹿在河边饮水，两个猎人正在拉弓射鹿，河边有装载物品的船只，房舍内几个女子在弹奏乐器，生动地反映出现实生活中的情趣。

3 释迦牟尼佛

清
长74、宽51厘米
内蒙古自治区包头市废旧回收公司征集

Buddha Sakyamuni
Qing Dynasty
Length: 74 cm, Width: 51cm

为佛传图组画之一。画面以众多的人物，复杂的构图，极为细腻
的绘制手法描绘了释迦牟尼的一生中重要的八件大事。色彩中应
用了大量金色，使画面色彩协调，是一幅精美唐卡作品。

4 释迦牟尼佛

清
长59.5、宽42.5厘米
内蒙古自治区包头市废旧回收公司征集

Buddha Sakyamuni
Qing Dynasty
Length: 59.5cm, Width: 42.5 cm

释迦牟尼结跏趺坐，持钵居中，背光后伞盖、鲜花，彩云中伎乐天女
唱赞，左右菩萨、弟子胁侍，下方信众手持宝物向佛顶礼供奉。

5 无量光佛

清

长61.3、宽36厘米

内蒙古自治区包头市废旧回收公司征集

Amitabha

Qing Dynasty

Length: 61.3cm, Width: 36cm

也称阿弥陀佛，无边光佛，藏传佛教称为月巴墨佛，是佛教西方极乐世界的创造
者。佛装红肤，双手持钵，两侧为菩萨侍从，上方释迦及两位大德人物，下方为尊
胜佛母、吉祥天母。

132

6 无量寿佛

清

长75、宽52厘米

内蒙古自治区包头市废旧回收公司征集

Amitayus Buddha

Qing Dynasty

Length: 75 cm, Width: 52cm

画面主尊绘无量寿佛，上方绘白度母、密集金刚、时轮金刚；下方
绘大威德金刚、降阎魔尊、六臂玛哈嘎拉，是典型的唐卡构图。画
面虽脱色，但人物绘制细腻，色彩协调，是唐卡中的精品。

7 无量寿佛

清

长73.5、宽46厘米

内蒙古自治区包头市废旧回收公司征集

Amitayus Buddha

Qing Dynasty

Length: 73.5 cm, Width: 46cm

无量寿佛是梵语"阿弥陀佛"的意译，汉传佛教无量寿佛与阿弥陀佛是同一尊佛，而藏传佛教分为佛装和菩萨装的不同两尊佛，也是最为崇奉的佛之一。其形象为结跏趺坐，头戴宝冠，双手结定印于双膝上，手心托长寿宝瓶。

135

8 龙尊王佛

清
长75.5、宽51厘米
内蒙古自治区包头市废旧回收公司征集

Nageshvaraja
Qing Dynasty
Length: 75.5 cm, Width: 51cm

主尊蓝肤结跏趺坐，头部的七条蛇（龙）是其标志，龙尊王全称"龙神上尊王佛"，
是佛教礼仪活动中称颂的三十五佛之一，主要在龙宫弘法，供奉他可以免于龙族加
害。画面上方为释迦牟尼佛、骑吼观音、弥勒、文殊；下方池中碧波荡漾，八个龙女
向佛礼敬，岸上鲜花盛开，菩萨、弟子分坐两旁，祥云缭绕，一派祥和景象。

9 普慧宏光佛

清
长42.2、宽28厘米
内蒙古自治区包头市废旧回收公司征集

Buddha of Brilliant Light

Qing Dynasty
Length: 42.2 cm, Width: 28cm

普慧宏光佛，四面，结跏趺坐，双手持轮。

10 四臂观音
清
长92.2、宽61.5厘米
内蒙古自治区包头市废旧回收公司征集

Four-armed Avalokiteshvara
Qing Dynasty
Length: 92.2 cm, Width: 61.5 cm

观音不同造型之一。四臂观音是西藏的守护神，也是藏传佛教最
为崇奉的菩萨之一，与文殊、金刚手合称"三怙主"，藏语称
"奇木格"。

11 千手千眼观音

清

长53.2、宽35.3厘米

内蒙古自治区包头市废旧回收公司征集

Sanasrabhuja-sahasranetra-avalokitesvara
Qing Dynasty
Length: 53.2 cm, Width: 35.3 cm

密宗六观音之一。据佛经讲，观音菩萨曾发誓要普度众生，长出千手千眼，千手表示维护众生，法力无边，千眼表示观照世间，有无穷的智慧和能力。四十二只手臂每只手掌中长出一只眼睛，除去主体的两只手臂，余下的四十只手，各配以"二十五有"，成为"千手千眼观音菩萨"。

12 十一面观音

清

长45、宽31厘米

内蒙古自治区包头市废旧回收公司征集

Eleven-faced Avalokitesvara

Qing Dynasty

Length: 45 cm, Width: 31 cm

众多观音之一,主救济,破修罗道,给众生以除病、灭罪,求福现世利益,总之为除恶向善。画面上方为宗喀巴师徒三尊,下方为黄财神、白度母、绿度母。

13 四臂观音

清
长49、宽35.6厘米
内蒙古自治区包头市废旧回收公司征集

Four-armed Avalokiteshvara
Qing Dynasty
Length: 49 cm, Width: 35.6 cm

为坐式的四臂观音，白色的身体代表清净无瑕，前两掌合胸前持如意宝珠，后两臂高
举至肩，右后手持念珠代表救度众生出离轮回，左手持白莲，代表净化一切烦恼。下
方为文殊、金刚手菩萨，合称"三怙主"。

14 文殊菩萨

清

长54.5、宽36.5厘米

内蒙古自治区包头市废旧回收公司征集

Manjushri Bodhisattva of Wisdom

Qing Dynasty

Length: 54.5 cm, Width: 36.5 cm

音译为文殊师利，意译为妙吉祥，藏语称"嘉木样"，为佛教四大菩萨之一，以辩才、
智慧第一，其道场在五台山。造像中以骑狮为多，而藏传佛教文殊除以骑狮，手持利
剑、经函外，还有多种不同造型。本唐卡以木刻板画印墨线，丝绢绘制，设色淡薄，周
边为金刚界、胎藏界不同的文殊造型，上方正中宗喀巴传为文殊菩萨化身。文殊左右五
座平顶山，象征五台山。

15 尊胜佛母

清
长87、宽59厘米
内蒙古自治区包头市废旧回收公司征集

Ushnishavijaya
Qing Dynasty
Length: 87cm, Width: 59 cm

三面八臂，额上有一眼，手中托化佛，持绳索、弓、金刚杵、净瓶等，
她也是一位救苦救难的女性菩萨。尊胜佛母与无量寿佛、白度母往往组
合一起，称为"长寿三尊"，成为吉祥福寿的尊像。

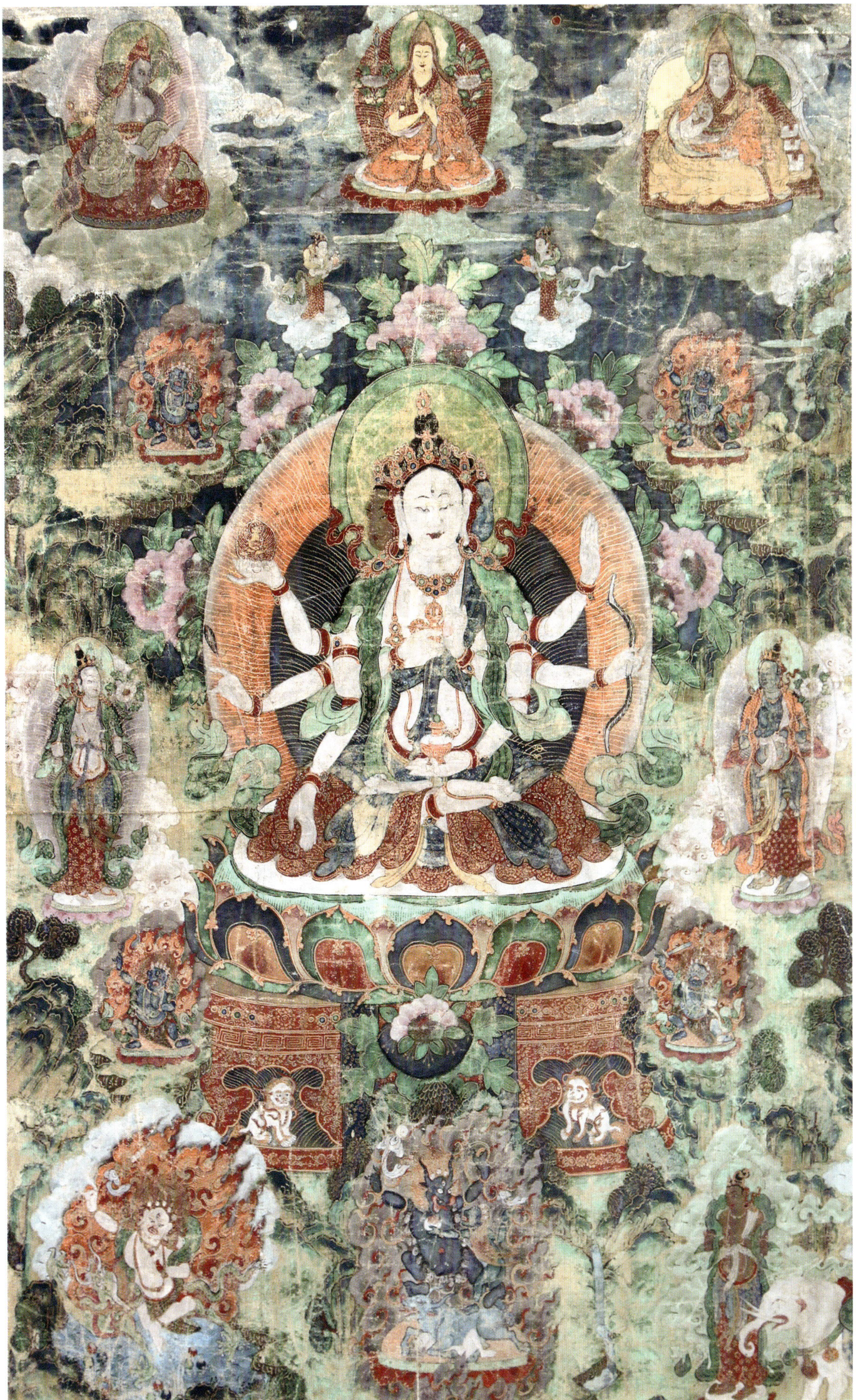

16 绿度母

清
长63.5、宽48厘米
内蒙古自治区包头市废旧回收公司征集

Green Tara

Qing Dynasty
Length: 63.5 cm, Width: 48 cm

度母又称"多罗"，藏语称"卓玛"，是藏传佛教女神，相传度母是观音眼泪幻化而成。以颜色区分为二十一尊，绿度母是最受信徒崇拜的女菩萨之一。舒坐于莲台上，双手持莲。其周边为不同造型的二十一尊度母。据称绿度母能使人摆脱八种灾难，所以又称"救八难度母"。相传文成公主是绿度母的化身。

17 白度母

清

长61、宽49厘米

内蒙古自治区包头市废旧回收公司征集

White Tara

Qing Dynasty

Length: 61 cm, Width: 49 cm

白度母是最受信徒崇拜的女菩萨之一。此幅唐卡中的白度母结跏趺坐，手持莲花，身有七眼。蒙古语称"查干多罗"，相传松赞干布的尼泊尔妃子尺尊公主是白度母的化身。

18 宗喀巴

清
长67、宽44.2厘米
内蒙古自治区包头市废旧回收公司征集

Tsongkha-pa

Qing Dynasty
Length: 67 cm, Width: 44.2cm

画面描绘宗喀巴在藏区传教，上方为文殊菩萨、龙树六庄严论师等人物。宗喀巴(1357～1419年)，西藏格鲁派(黄教)创始人。本名罗桑扎巴，青海宗喀(今湟中)人。宗喀巴三岁时受近事戒，七岁出家，十六岁进藏。针对当时戒律松弛，力求纠正各教派的流弊，宗喀巴决意进行宗教改革。主张学经要注重修习次第，循序渐进。先显宗后密宗。明洪武二十一年(1388年)，他和弟子改戴黄色僧帽，以重视戒律为号召，被称为黄帽派。永乐七年（1409年）初，宗喀巴在拉萨发起大祈愿法会，并在拉萨东北创建了甘丹寺，以噶当派教义为基础，正式建立格鲁派。主要著作有《菩提道次第广论》、《密宗道次第广论》等。

19 宗喀巴师徒三尊

清

长50、宽34厘米

内蒙古自治区包头市废旧回收公司征集

Tsongkha-pa and pupils

Qing Dynasty

Length: 50 cm, Width: 34cm

画面中部宗喀巴师徒三尊盘坐于云海之中，上方象征弥勒
菩萨兜率天宫，下方为僧人供奉。

20 宗喀巴集会树

清
长77、宽51.5厘米
内蒙古自治区包头市废旧回收公司征集

Tsongkha-pa assembly tree
Qing Dynasty
Length: 77 cm, Width: 51.5 cm

又称"皈依境",是佛教信徒作为聚集资粮、礼拜供养的对象。画面中海里长出一颗如意宝树,树上画有上百尊菩萨、护法等尊像,宗喀巴位于树顶端,身后是历代祖师、大德。黄教寺院通常都供奉此图。

21 阿底峡大师
清
长82、宽51.5厘米
内蒙古自治区包头市废旧回收公司征集

Atisha
Qing Dynasty
Length: 82 cm, Width: 51.5 cm

画面上几乎密不透风地绘满各种人物、建筑，主要描绘了阿底峡大师不畏艰险，从古印度越过雪山，在雪域传播佛教的故事。阿底峡（982~1054年），古印度高僧（今孟加拉国达卡地区人）。曾任印度著名的那烂陀寺、超戒寺住持。公元1038年受阿里王子降曲沃之请进藏传教，并译经授徒。著有《菩提道灯论》等五十余部论著和《医头术》等医学著作，成为西藏后弘期佛教发展的重要人物，1054年圆寂于前藏纳塘寺。其弟子仲敦巴弘传其学术，发展成为噶当派。

22 兜率天上师瑜伽法

清

长66、宽40.2厘米

内蒙古自治区包头市废旧回收公司征集

Guru in Tusita heaven with a posture of Yogasana

Qing Dynasty

Length: 66 cm, Width: 40.2cm

画面中心师徒三尊端坐于祥云之上，上方为弥勒菩萨兜率
天宫，下方为弟子虔诚供奉。

23 萨班·贡嘎坚赞

清

长65、宽39厘米

内蒙古自治区包头市废旧回收公司征集

Sarbanes · Gongga Gyaltsen

Qing Dynasty

Length: 65 cm, Width: 39 cm

画面正中绘萨迦派第四祖萨班的青年形象，英俊潇洒，身着杏黄色袈裟，戴圆顶法帽，右臂抬起，左臂伸出作辩经姿态，神情安详。画面左上角天空绘修行本尊文殊菩萨，右上角是上师扎巴坚赞，左下角绘四臂大黑天，右下角绘被降伏的外道者听其传教。

168

24 香巴拉国王

清
长64、宽40厘米
内蒙古自治区包头市废旧回收公司征集

King of Shambhala
Qing Dynasty
Length: 64cm, Width: 40 cm

画面中主尊人物的装束、坐姿表明是香巴拉某位国王。香巴拉
是藏传佛教所宣传的北方极乐世界，有二十五代国王热心的护
法。其上方为时轮金刚，穿黑衣者为皈依佛法的异教徒，国王
似在向其宣扬时轮金刚法。

25 克主杰尊者

清
长52.5、宽37.5厘米
内蒙古自治区包头市废旧回收公司征集

Arya
Qing Dynasty
Length: 52.5 cm, Width: 37.5 cm

主尊为宗喀巴弟子克主杰·格雷贝桑，下方黑底金字为赞颂词。克主杰·格雷贝桑，明洪武十八年（1385年）诞生于后藏拉堆多雄的曲沃。童年时在萨迦寺出家，拜萨迦派僧格坚赞为师，受沙弥戒。之后，又从吉尊热蓬娃学习密宗。18岁到前藏听宗喀巴讲经。宗喀巴向克主杰讲说"三藏"，授大灌顶。克主杰对宗喀巴的渊博知识深感钦佩，遂跟随宗喀巴在藏区传教，后被追认为第一世班禅额尔德尼活佛。

ༀ་།ཀྱེ་རྒྱལ་བ་ཀུན་གྱི་ཡེ་ཤེས་ཉིད་དུ་གྱུར། །ལོ་པཎ་རྒྱ་མཚོ་ཆུ་བོ་འདུས་པ་ཡི། ༀ་།ཡང་དག་དོན་ལ་ཐོགས་མེད་མཁྱེན་རབ་ཆེ། །རྒྱལ་བསྟན་མདོ་སྔགས་བཤད་སྒྲུབ་རྒྱ་མཚོ་ཆེ། ། བེ་རོ་ཙ་ན་ཙ།

26 财神毗沙门天

清
长66、宽43厘米
内蒙古自治区包头市废旧回收公司征集

Vaishravana
Qing Dynasty
Length: 66 cm, Width: 43 cm

毗沙门天，蒙古语称"那木斯莱"，为四大天王之一的北
方守护神，同时也作为财神专门保护众生财富，颇受尊
崇。他身金色，骑白狮，右手持伞，左手抱鼠，鼠口中吐
宝，象征财富。

174

27 八大佛塔

清

长60、宽41厘米

内蒙古自治区包头市废旧回收公司征集

Eight stupa

Qing Dynasty

Length: 60 cm, Width: 41 cm

八大佛塔是纪念释迦牟尼一生的主要八件大事，即聚莲塔，纪念释迦牟尼诞生；菩提塔，纪念释迦牟尼菩提树下成道；吉祥塔，纪念释迦牟尼初转法轮；神变塔，纪念释迦牟尼降伏外道；天降塔，纪念释迦牟尼升天为说法重返人间；和解塔，纪念释迦牟尼说服众僧避免另立宗派；胜利塔，纪念释迦牟尼战胜恶魔；涅槃塔，纪念释迦牟尼圆寂。

28 无量寿佛曼陀罗

清
长56、宽38厘米
内蒙古自治区包头市废旧回收公司征集

Amitayus Mandala
Qing Dynasty
Length: 56 cm, Width: 38 cm

曼陀罗也称曼达，梵文意译为坛场，是密宗修法的法器。曼陀罗内聚集着佛、菩萨。本曼陀罗为无量寿佛曼陀罗，供曼陀罗是积聚福德与智慧最圆满的方法。曼陀罗是僧人和藏民日常修习秘法时的"心中宇宙图"，共有四种，即所谓的"四曼为相"，一般是以外圆内方为主，图案形式相对称，中心为城居住着本尊。

PLATE 1 CONTENTS OF THANGKAS

图版·唐卡

29 战神

清

长56.8、宽35厘米

内蒙古自治区包头市废旧回收公司征集

God of War

Qing Dynasty

Length: 56.8 cm, Width: 35 cm

骑白马，身挎弓箭，全身铠甲，中国武士装束，右手持鞭，
亦称"白马天神"。据说蒙古族信奉此神，可免除草原牲畜
的疫病，保五畜兴旺。

30 吉祥天母

清
长51、宽35厘米
内蒙古自治区包头市废旧回收公司征集

Palden Lhamo

Qing Dynasty
Length: 51cm, Width: 35 cm

藏名"班达拉姆",是女性护法神,呈忿怒形。其形象为肤色青蓝的凶神,怒发竖立,头戴骷髅冠,头顶有半月和孔雀毛。右边耳朵上有小狮子为饰,据说象征着听经;左耳上挂着小蛇,意为忿怒。腰上挂着账簿,为专门记载人们所作坏事的档案,恶人将来要受剥皮处置。她左手拿的骷髅棒是专门对付恶鬼阿修罗的,右手端着盛满鲜血的骷髅碗。身上披着人皮,那人皮据说是她亲生儿子的,象征大义灭亲。骑的黄骡子臀有一眼,在马鞍前端下方有两个红白骰子,红的主杀,白的主教化。鞍子后有一个荷包袋,里面盛着疫病毒菌,也就是说她是主生死、病瘟、善恶的神。

32 乃琼事业王法器

清
长342、宽36厘米
内蒙古自治区包头市废旧回收公司征集

Ritual Implement of King of Career
Qing Dynasty
Length: 342 cm, Width: 36 cm

画面中心为乃琼、善金刚、门普布查等护法尊像外形，而无真身。两侧绘牛、马、羊、驼、八吉祥、七珍宝、乐器等。背景山峦起伏，以骷髅、人肠、人皮组成的璎珞非常恐怖。这种唐卡多张挂在护法神殿，以威慑魔敌。

31 六臂大白勇保护法

清
长46、宽31厘米
内蒙古自治区包头市废旧回收公司征集

Six-armed White Mahakala
Qing Dynasty
Length: 46cm, Width: 31 cm

亦称白玛哈嘎拉，藏语"贡格勒"。身白色，一面六臂三目，呈忿怒
形，手拿各种法器。脚下踩吉祥王菩萨（八大镇方守土神之一），象
征着国土安宁，守土镇方。白玛哈嘎拉周边黄、红、绿、白色空行母
为其护从。

33 大红勇保护法

清
长45、宽32厘米
内蒙古自治区包头市废旧回收公司征集

Red Mahakala
Qing Dynasty
Length: 45 cm, Width: 32cm

护法神之一，左手持矛、弓，手抓血红人心欲送入口中。右手举
剑，红肤面相凶恶，脚踏俘获的异教徒和绿马，周边为其护从。

34 六臂玛哈嘎拉

清

长52、宽34厘米

内蒙古自治区包头市废旧回收公司征集

Six-armed Mahakala

Qing Dynasty

Length: 52cm, Width: 34 cm

此尊又称六臂大黑天，梵名"玛哈嘎拉"，"玛哈"为"大"，"嘎拉"为"黑"，藏语称"贡普"，是古印度的军神、战神。民间视其为施福之神，佛经认为他是大日如来为降伏恶魔而化现的形象。玛哈嘎拉有二臂、四臂、六臂多种形象，是藏密重要护法神。身蓝黑，面相凶恶，六臂手拿法器，身披白象皮，腰系虎皮裙，脚踩象王。象王手持萝卜正在向其贡献。据称供奉此神可增威德，举事能胜。

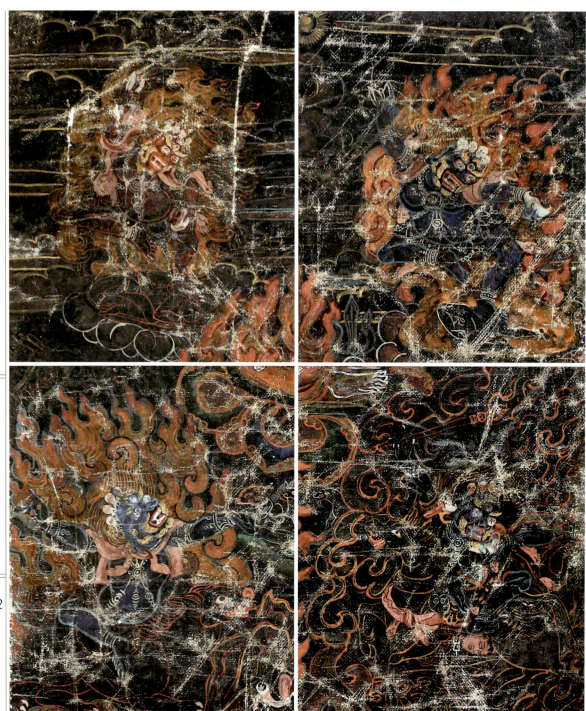

35 六臂玛哈嘎拉

清

长60、宽44厘米

内蒙古自治区包头市废旧回收公司征集

Six-armed Mahakala

Qing Dynasty

Length: 60 cm, Width: 44cm

本唐卡绘画风格独特，以黑色为主调，间以其他色彩点缀，色调分明，装饰浓郁。此唐卡亦称"黑唐"。

36 胜乐金刚

清
长61、宽49厘米
内蒙古自治区包头市废旧回收公司征集

Chakrasamvara

Qing Dynasty
Length: 61 cm, Width: 49cm

藏语称"登巧",蒙古语称"德穆钦格",为藏密尊奉的五大本尊之一。此尊的形象十分复杂,全身特征都具有象征意义。身青色,四面各三目,头戴骷髅冠,顶髻有摩尼宝,以半月为饰,下着虎皮裙,有十二只手,象征克服十二种缘起的方法。主臂左手持金刚铃,右手持金刚杵,两手同时抱明妃金刚亥母。明妃一面二臂,面呈红色,有三只眼,戴骷髅冠,右手拿月形刀,左手拿人头骨碗,献与本尊。明妃的两腿姿势很特别,左腿伸,与主尊右腿并齐,右腿盘在主尊腰间,这也是辨别这一本尊的重要特征。胜乐金刚另有二十四臂形象。

37 时轮金刚

清

长63.2、宽42厘米

内蒙古自治区包头市废旧回收公司征集

Kalachakra

Qing Dynasty

Length: 63.2cm, Width: 42 cm

藏名为"堆柯",蒙古语称"丁科尔",意为"时轮"。相传古印度北方有香巴拉国,国王月善最早弘传时轮金刚法。时轮金刚认为一切众生都在过去、现在、未来"三时"的"迷界"之中,并以时轮表示"三时"。时轮金刚双身合抱,男体为四头二十四臂,女体为单头八臂,每只手都持有不同法器,脚下踏人,表降伏意。上方为宗喀巴师徒三尊,下方为吐蕃赞普松赞干布、赤松德赞、赤热巴巾,藏语称"却结弥王郎松",意为祖孙三代法王。西藏前弘期佛教发展与这三位法王支持密切相关。

38 大威德金刚

清
长60、宽44.3厘米
内蒙古自治区包头市废旧回收公司征集

Yamantaka
Qing Dynasty
Length: 60 cm, Width: 44.3cm

大威德金刚，因其能降服恶魔，故称大威，又有护善之功，故又称大德，梵名"阎曼德迦"，藏语为"多吉久谢"，意为"怖畏金刚"，民间称牛头明王。藏密认为是文殊菩萨的忿怒相，大威德的形象有很多种，常见有二臂、四臂、十八臂、三十四臂等。有单体的，也有双身的，其中，最能代表其修法的是三十四臂双身形象，这也是其最复杂、最恐怖的一种。其怀中拥抱的明妃罗浪杂娃，也是一脸恶相。明王代表慈悲，明妃代表智慧，他们的结合代表"悲智合一"。

内蒙古包头博物馆馆藏岩画百余幅，书中所收51幅，主要采集于内蒙古自治区包头市的达茂旗、巴彦淖尔市的乌拉特中旗和阿拉善盟的阿拉善左旗及阿拉善右旗四个地区。岩画的时代从新石器时代至清代。内容包括动物、人物、狩猎、放牧、车辆与道路、动物蹄印、巫师、人面像、太阳神、怪兽等。岩画的制作方法有磨刻、凿刻和划刻。

岩画的内容与当地的自然环境和经济状态有着千丝万缕的联系。包头的达茂草原适宜畜牧业发展，因此，家畜、放牧以及与畜牧经济有关的蹄印崇拜成为该地区岩画的主要特征，表现出浓厚的畜牧经济色彩。巴彦淖尔市乌拉特中旗既有山地又有草原，适合于畜牧经济和狩猎经济同时经营，岩画内容多表现畜牧与狩猎两大主题。阿拉善地区属荒漠草原、戈壁和沙漠环境，生活在这里的人们为了适应恶劣环境，需要不断地迁徙，以达到"逐水草而居"的目的，因此，有相当多的岩画表现了迁徙的场面。另外，也有一部分岩画表现的是能够适应沙漠环境的骆驼形象。

51 pieces of rock paintings aged from Neolithic Age to Qing Dynasty from more than 100 collections of Baotou Museum are included in this catalogue. These rock paintings with methods of polishing, chiseling and carving are collected from Damao Banner in Baotou City, Wulate Middle Banner of Bayan Nur, Alxa Left Banner of Alxa and Alxa Right Banner. The contents of these rock paintings are animals, human beings, hunting, herding, chariots and roads, hoof prints, wizards, faces, sun-gods, monster, etc.

The contents of rock paintings have countless ties to local natural environment and economic form. The Damao steppe is very suitable to the development of stock farming, that is the reason why domestic animals, herding and the worship of hoof print related to herding economy are the principal character of the rock paintings in this area. Mountain land and grassland, where are fit to the operation of herding and hunting economy, can be easily found in Wulate Middle Banner, Bayan Nur, and that explains the two themes: animal husbandry and hunting. The desert steppe, gobi and desert in Alxa area result in the continually migration of local people to adapt to the terrible environment and maintain the lifestyle of living where there is water and grass, and that lead to the scene of migration and the images of camel in the rock paintings.

岩　画

CONTENTS OF ROCK PAINTINGS

包头市
巴彦淖尔市
阿拉善盟

BAO TOU
BAYAN NUR
ALXA LEAGUE

1 人面像

新石器时代
画面高57、宽38厘米
内蒙古自治区包头市达尔罕茂明安联合旗推喇嘛庙采集

Face
Neolithic Age
Height: 57cm, Width: 38cm

磨刻制作。主体画面为正面猴脸形人面像，图案古朴凝
重、充满神秘色彩，反映了古人对神灵的崇拜。

203

2 牵马图

春秋战国
画面高52、宽52厘米
内蒙古自治区包头市达尔罕茂明安联合旗推喇嘛庙采集

Horse-leading

Spring and Autumn – Warring States Period
Height: 52cm, Width: 52cm

凿刻后打磨。主体画面为一人牵一马，人呈正面形象立于马前，系尾饰，马立于画面中央，造型生动流畅，马蹄下刻有蹄印，以表现图案的三维效果。

3 神话动物

春秋战国
画面高26、宽40厘米
内蒙古自治区包头市达尔罕茂明安联合旗推喇嘛庙采集

The mythical creature
Spring and Autumn – Warring States Period
Height: 26cm, Width: 40cm

凿刻后打磨。动物呈侧身伫立状，身体由马头、鹰喙、牛身组成，动物的颈部粗壮，颈上部隆起，尾巴纤细，雄性特征明显，体型具有牛的特征，造型雄健丰腴。

4 神话动物

春秋战国
画面高26、宽40厘米
内蒙古自治区包头市达尔罕茂明安联合旗推喇嘛庙采集

The mythical creature

Spring and Autumn – Warring States Period
Height: 26cm, Width: 40cm

凿刻后打磨。动物呈侧身伫立状，身体为马的造型，但
在马的面颊上刻有两只角，由前额至颈部刻有一只角，
类似羊角。

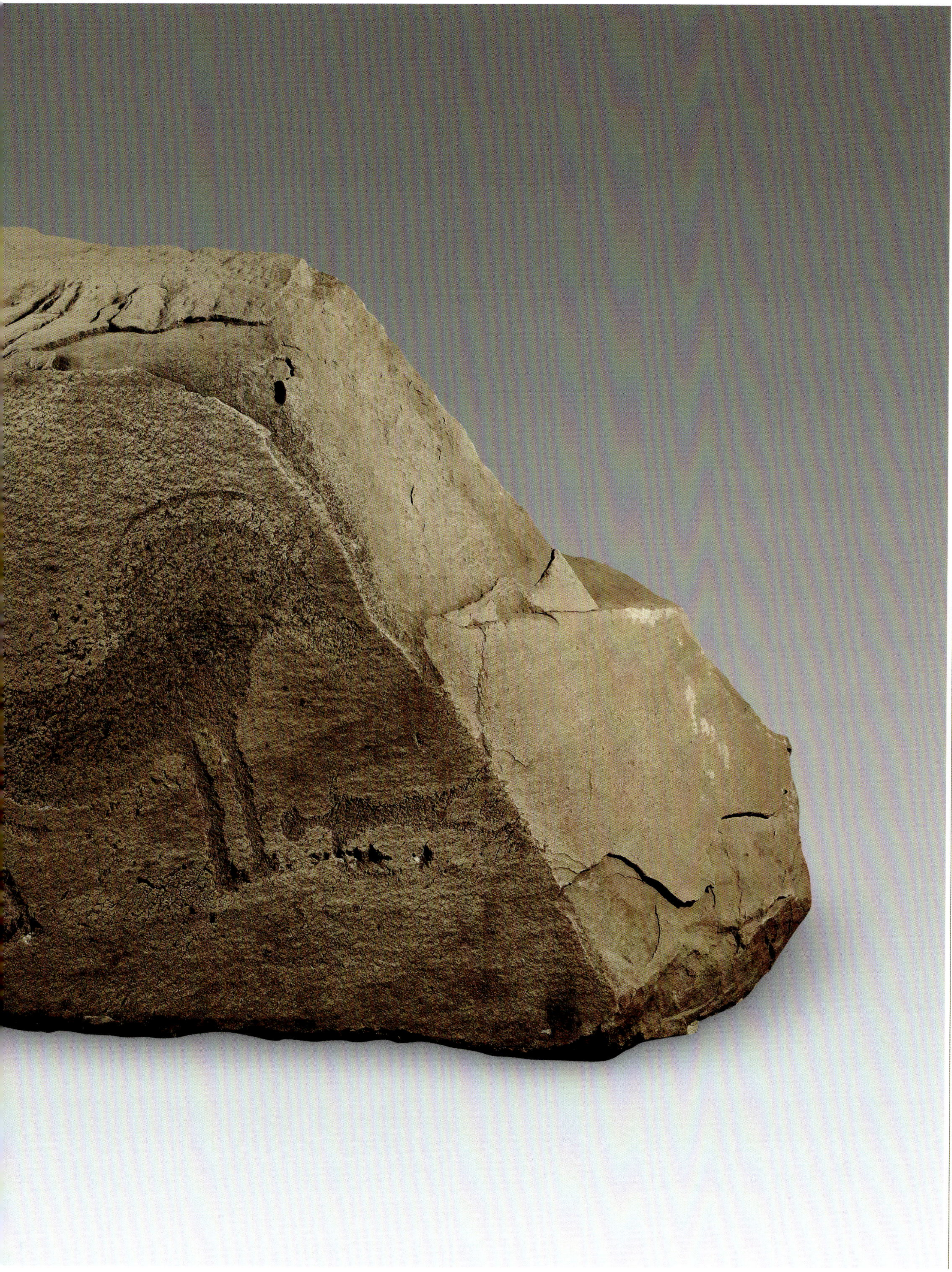

5 车辆·道路·动物

春秋战国
画面高30、宽76厘米
内蒙古自治区包头市达尔罕茂明安联合旗推喇嘛庙采集

Chariot · Road · Animal

Spring and Autumn – Warring States Period
Height: 30cm, Width: 76cm

凿刻制作。画面中部由左至右刻有四条车辙印，以表示
道路，道路上下各有一套车马，车为单辕、圆形舆、双
轮，两马驾辕。

6 神话动物

春秋战国
画面高41、宽23厘米
内蒙古自治区包头市达尔罕茂明安联合旗推喇嘛庙采集

The mythical creature
Spring and Autumn – Warring States Period
Height: 41cm, Width: 23cm

凿刻制作。主体画面为三只动物，上面一只属羊的形态，但尾部残缺，无法判断其尾部属于哪种动物的尾部。按照一般规律，岩画中羊的尾部是向上翻卷的，从图形上看，该图案画的并非羊尾，因此推断它应是组合式神话动物。中部的动物和下面的动物明显属于组合式神话动物，特别是下面的动物特征更为明显，头、角都是羊的特征，身体、四肢、尾、蹄印是马的特征，属羊与马的组合动物。在三只神话动物中，有意突显了羊的大角，表现出画面内涵的重要意义，即作画者刻画的是神兽，并非一般动物。

7 鹿

春秋战国
画面高34、宽52厘米
内蒙古自治区包头市达尔罕茂明安联合旗推喇嘛庙采集

Deer
Spring and Autumn – Warring States Period
Height: 34cm, Width: 52cm

凿刻后打磨。鹿的身体修长，侧身伫立，目视远方。画面
简洁传神，刻画了鹿天生胆小、警惕和机敏的特性。

216

8 双鹿

春秋战国
画面高73、宽30厘米
内蒙古自治区包头市达尔罕茂明安联合旗推喇嘛庙采集

Double deers
Spring and Autumn – Warring States Period
Height: 73cm, Width: 30cm

凿刻后打磨。主体图案为上下排列的两只梅花鹿，鹿呈
侧身伫立状，头向一致，上面一只鹿头上长角，生殖器
挺举，为雄鹿，下面一只无角，为雌鹿。

9 动物群

战国
画面高43、宽69厘米
内蒙古自治区包头市达尔罕茂明安联合旗推喇嘛庙采集

Animal herd
Warring States Period
Height: 43cm, Width: 69cm

凿刻制作。画面内容包括羊、马、鹿、狼（或犬）等动物。各种动物造型准确写实、神态各异、充满活力，表现了草原上祥和、恬静的景象。

10 马·动物蹄印

战国—汉
画面高82、宽67厘米
内蒙古自治区包头市达尔罕茂明安联合旗推喇嘛庙采集

Horse·Hoof print
Warring States Period – Han Dynasty
Height: 82cm, Width: 67cm

凿刻制作。画面由一匹马和多个蹄印构成，马和蹄印均以线条勾勒出轮
廓。多为偶蹄类动物。动物蹄印是包头达茂岩画的一大特色，蹄印被牧人
当做家畜的主要标识。古人认为，将蹄印凿刻在岩石上，通过巫师作法操
作后，就可以达到六畜兴旺、牛羊成群的目的。

11 虎·动物蹄印

战国—汉
画面高70、宽120厘米
内蒙古自治区包头市达尔罕茂明安联合旗推喇嘛庙采集

Tiger·Hoof print
Warring States Period – Han Dynasty
Height: 70cm, Width: 120cm

凿刻制作。画面由虎、骑者、羊和多个动物蹄印构成。
画面中部为一只虎，虎的右侧为一骑者，上方为北山
羊，周边布满动物蹄印。画面中有叠压关系，不是同一
次作画。

顶部

224

12 人·马·羊

汉
画面高32、宽47厘米
内蒙古自治区包头市达尔罕茂明安联合旗推喇嘛庙采集

Person · Horse · Sheep
Han Dynasty
Height: 32cm, Width: 47cm

凿刻制作。画面内容包括巫师、北山羊和马等动物，两个巫师并排站立，两臂平伸，至肘部向下弯曲，两腿分开，生殖器外露，脚尖朝外，呈骑马蹲裆式，是典型的做法祈福动作。整幅岩画以线条形式构图，作画风格有向简略化、抽象化过渡的趋势。

13 牛·兽·太阳
汉
画面高33、宽48厘米
内蒙古自治区包头市达尔罕茂明安联合旗推喇嘛庙采集

Ox · Beast · Sun
Han Dynasty
Height: 33cm, Width: 48cm

凿刻制作。画面右侧为一头牛，中部为一圆环形图案，带有光芒，可能表示太阳。左侧为一只兽，头向与牛相反。

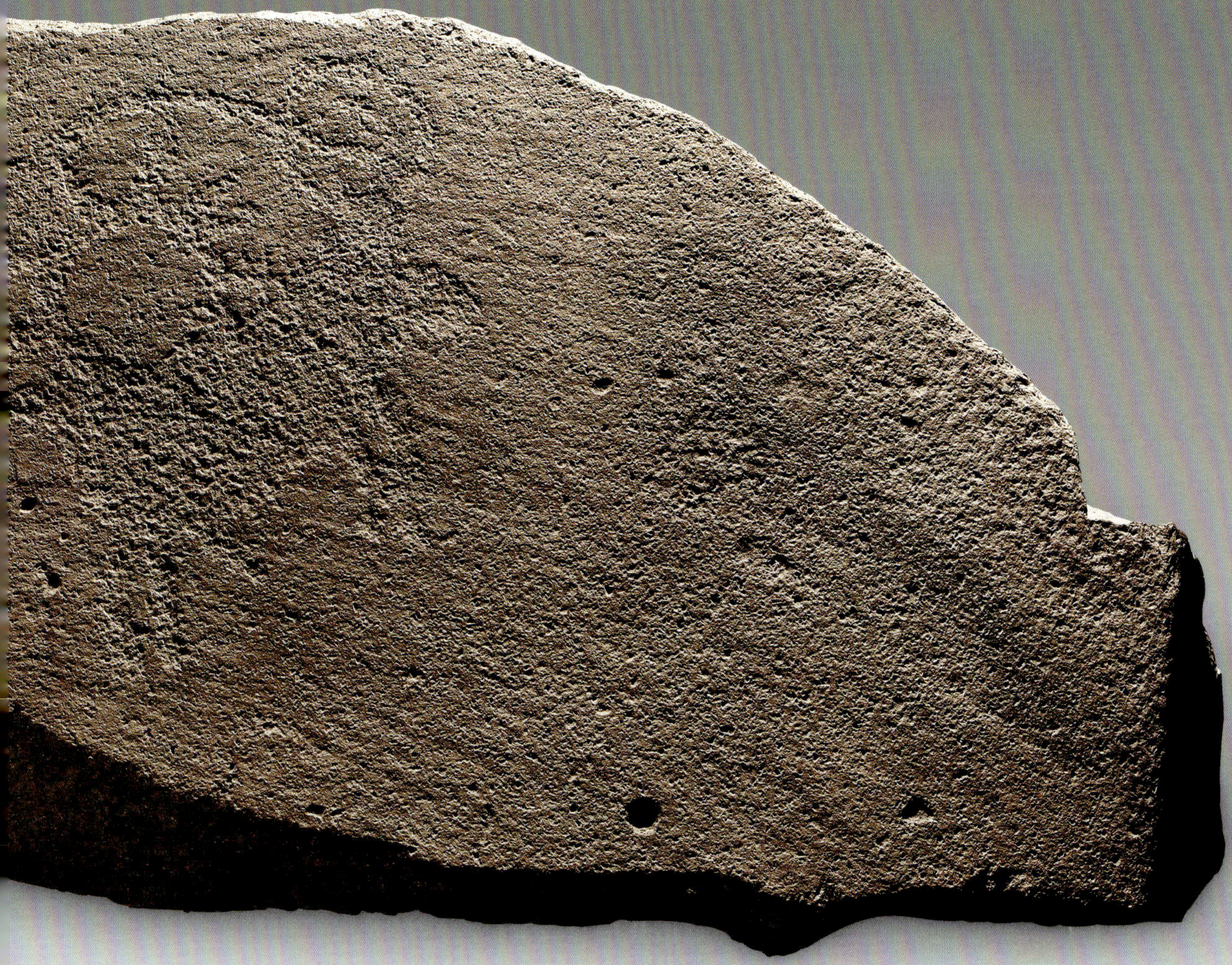

14 双人舞蹈

汉
画面高29、宽22厘米
内蒙古自治区包头市达尔罕茂明安联合旗推喇嘛庙采集

Double dance

Han Dynasty
Height: 29cm, Width: 22cm

凿刻制作。画面为两个站立的人形象，两人并排携手，两腿分开，左边一人
发辫（或头饰）双分下垂；右边一人单辫（或戴头饰）上立，系尾饰。两人
动作整齐划一，富有韵律，似作双人舞蹈动作。

15 抽象符号

北朝—唐
画面高43、宽72厘米
内蒙古自治区包头市达尔罕茂明安联合旗推喇嘛庙采集

Abstract symbol

Northern Dynasties – Tang Dynasty
Height: 43cm, Width: 72cm

凿刻制作。画面由众多抽象符号和一个弓形图案构成，其中可辨
识的在画面右侧有一只北山羊形象，抽象符号中个别符号与古突
厥文字母相似，岩画应为古突厥人所为。

232

16 北山羊群

商周
画面高68、宽73厘米
内蒙古自治区巴彦淖尔市乌拉特中旗温根镇几公海勒斯太东达哈门山采集

Capra ibex flock
Shang and Zhou Periods
Height: 68cm, Width: 73cm

凿刻后打磨。画面由多只北山羊构成，中部一只最有代表性，羊呈侧身伫立状，身体肥壮雄健，头昂起、吻前伸，羊角向后弯至背部，下颌长胡须，生殖器挺举。造型生动准确，充满动感，画面具象写实，代表了早期岩画的作画特征。

234

17 动物群

春秋战国
画面高44、宽72厘米
内蒙古自治区巴彦淖尔市乌拉特中旗温根镇几公海勒斯太东达哈门山采集

Fauna

Spring and Autumn – Warring States Period
Height: 44cm, Width: 72cm

凿刻制作。画面由一只鹿和多只北山羊组成。鹿刻于画面上方，呈侧身伫立状，身体和颈部细长，四条腿短且细，吻前伸，双耳直立。鹿角由头部一直向后伸至臀部附近，角枝是由一根主干向后延伸，主干上的枝节一致朝上整齐排列。画面的其他部分刻有一群北山羊，北山羊的造型风格与鹿基本一致。

18 狩猎

春秋战国
画面高51、宽103厘米
内蒙古自治区巴彦淖尔市乌拉特中旗温根镇几公海勒斯太东达哈门山采集

Hunting

Spring and Autumn – Warring States Period
Height: 51cm, Width: 103cm

凿刻制作。狩猎场面可分成四组：第一组位于画面中部上方，为一猎人手
举投标投向前方的梅花鹿，梅花鹿身体健壮，鹿角硕大华丽，呈奔跑状；
第二组位于第一组下方，为一猎人持弓搭箭，射中前方北山羊的臀部，北
山羊的背部已连中两标，留有标头；第三组位于画面左侧，为一猎人手持
弩机，射向前方的羊；第四组位于画面右侧，为一猎人手持弓箭，射向远
方的猎物。

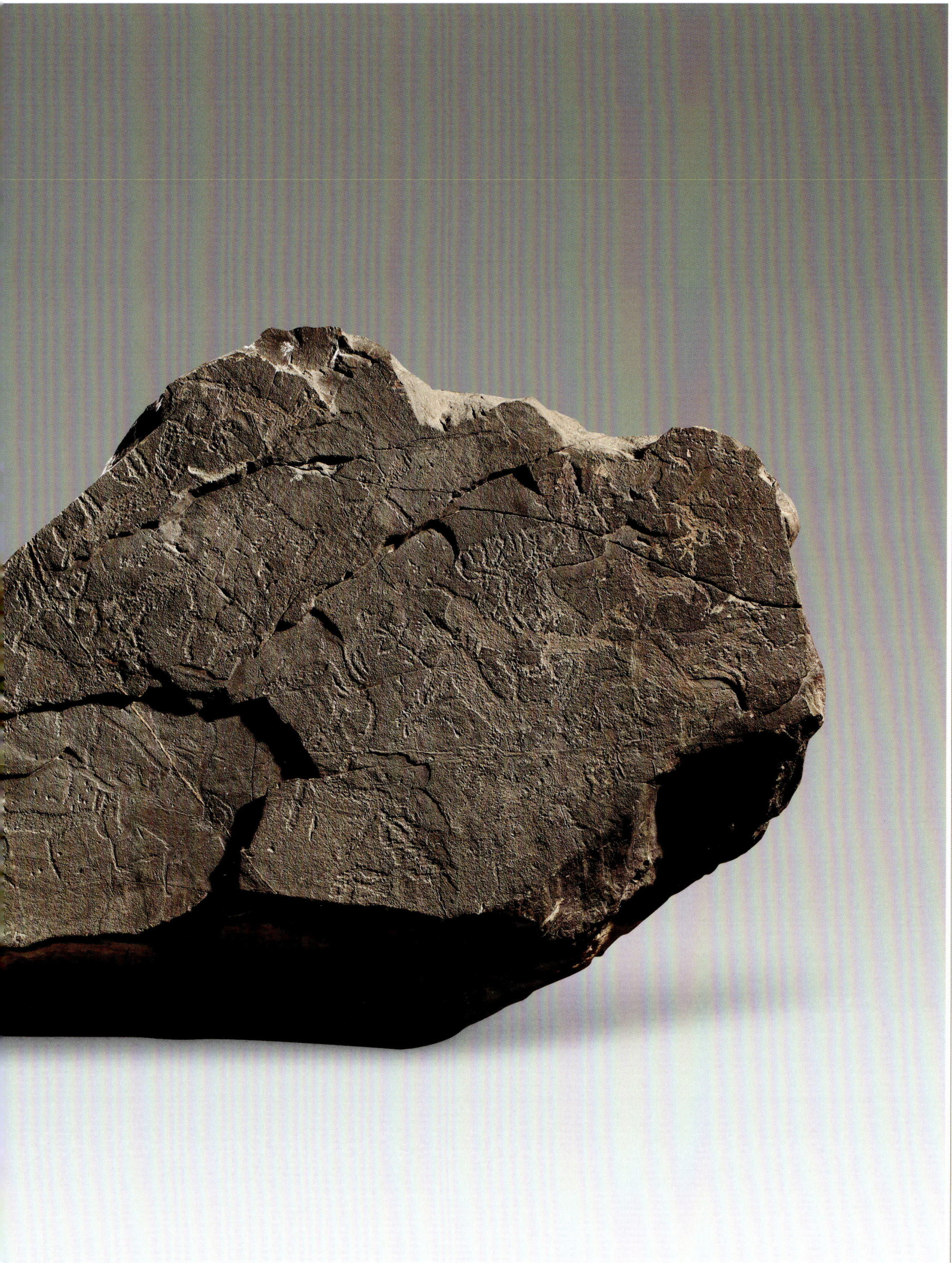

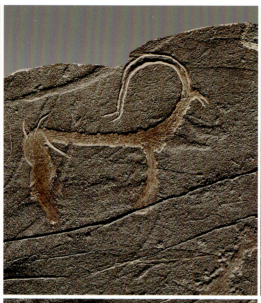

238

19 猎人·北山羊群

春秋战国、汉代、宋元
画面高29、宽50厘米
内蒙古自治区巴彦淖尔市乌拉特中旗温根镇几公海勒斯太东达哈门山采集

Hunter·C apra ibex flock

Spring and Autumn – Warring States Period, Han Dynasty, Song and Yuan
Dynasties
Height: 29cm, Width: 50cm

凿刻、划刻制作。位于画面上方的是两只北山羊和一个猎人，左边一只北
山羊侧身站立，造型具象，刻双角四腿，羊角夸张，尾上翻，生殖器裸
露。右边一只北山羊颜色较浅，呈侧身站立，刻两腿，羊角、生殖器、羊
尾为划刻。羊后有一猎人，持弓搭箭对准羊的臀部，为划刻，刻痕轻且
细，作画风格与羊截然不同，明显不是出自一人之手。画面中部为三只北
山羊横向排列，左边两只风格一致，侧身站立、体态较长，刻双角四腿，
右边一只北山羊无角，作画风格与左边两只不同，非一人刻成。最下方的
北山羊身体为凿刻，嘴、羊角、四腿为划刻，显然不是一次性作画。中部
画面为春秋战国时代作品，左上方和下方画面为汉代以后作品，右上方一
只北山羊和猎人的作画年代约宋元时期作品。

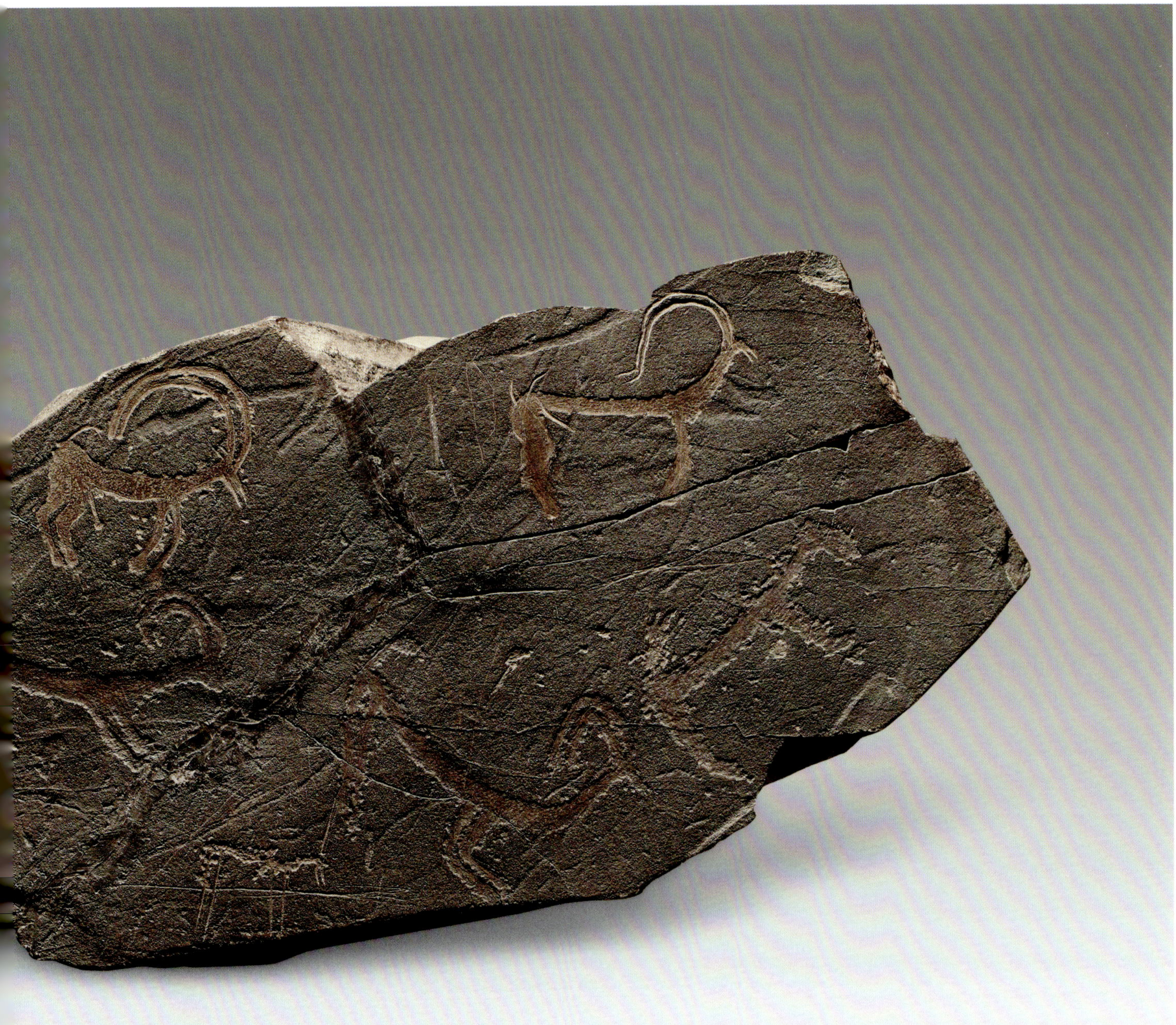

20 猎北山羊

春秋战国
画面高58、宽45厘米
内蒙古自治区巴彦淖尔市乌拉特中旗温根镇几公海勒斯太东达哈门山采集

Capra ibex - hunting

Spring and Autumn – Warring States Period
Height: 58cm, Width: 45cm

凿刻制作。画面为一持弓搭箭的猎人射中北山羊的头部，猎人的尾饰与羊的嘴部相连。北山羊侧身站立，羊角向后弯至臀部，十分夸张，羊刻有双尾，一尾向上翻卷，一尾向下弯曲。

21 群鹿

春秋战国
画面高50、宽33厘米
内蒙古自治区巴彦淖尔市乌拉特中旗温根镇几公海勒斯太东达哈门山采集

Deer herd

Spring and Autumn – Warring States Period
Height: 50cm, Width: 33cm

凿刻制作。画面由五只梅花鹿上下排列构成,四只头向朝右,一只头向朝左。最上面一只和最下面一只分别刻有鹿角,背上骑人,说明当时鹿已被驯养,并有骑鹿习俗。从上往下数第二只鹿的肚下有一只小鹿正在吃奶,活泼可爱。整幅画面表现了祥和的草原牧鹿景象。

22 猎狼

春秋战国
画面高31、宽56厘米
内蒙古自治区巴彦淖尔市乌拉特中旗温根镇几公海勒斯太东达哈门山采集

Wolf-hunting

Spring and Autumn – Warring States Period
Height: 31cm, Width: 56cm

凿刻制作。画面上部从右至左刻有马，马后尾随着狼，狼后有一猎人持弓对着狼，呈引弓待发之势。三者头向相同，前后尾随，可谓螳螂捕蝉黄雀在后。画面中部为一只北山羊和一匹马，马和北山羊有叠压关系，说明这两个形象不是一次性作画。整幅画面生动自然、妙趣横生。

23 神话动物
战国
画面高24、宽14厘米
内蒙古自治区巴彦淖尔市乌拉特中旗温根镇几公海勒斯太东达哈门山采集

The mythical creature
Warring States Period
Height: 24cm, Width: 14cm

凿刻制作。画面以线条凿刻出羊的身体轮廓，呈昂首侧身站立状，吻前伸，颈上挺，尾上卷，身体敦厚。画面以盘羊为基本形态，头顶上用四条线勾画出四只角，羊角呈同心圆形状，十分夸张。作画线条自然流畅，造型生动活泼。

24 骑者

战国
画面高31、宽66厘米
内蒙古自治区巴彦淖尔市乌拉特中旗温根镇几公海勒斯太采集

Rider

Warring States Period
Height: 31cm, Width: 66cm

凿刻制作。主体画面为三个骑马者，上方两个骑者图形较小、侧身、头向一致、前后相随，马的形态具象写实，无鞍具。中部图形较大，马呈侧身站立，作画以线条先刻出身体轮廓，身体中间凿点稀疏。马的面部较长，刻双耳四腿，无鞍具，马背上骑坐的人比例较小。

25 猎羊·梅花鹿

战国
画面高68、宽29厘米
内蒙古自治区巴彦淖尔市乌拉特中旗温根镇几公海勒斯太采集

Goat-hunting · Spotted deer
Warring States Period
Height: 68cm, Width: 29cm

凿刻制作。画面上方是一只侧身站立的梅花鹿，鹿的身体修长，角枝华丽，刻画出鹿胆小、谨慎、机敏、善跑的特性。鹿的下方是一猎人手持弓箭，对准前方的北山羊准备射击。

26 梅花鹿

战国
画面高24、宽28厘米
内蒙古自治区巴彦淖尔市乌拉特中旗温根镇几公海勒斯太采集

Spotted deer
Warring States Period
Height: 24cm, Width: 28cm

鹿侧身站立，作画先以线条凿刻出身体轮廓，在轮廓内填凿小圆
点以表示鹿身上的斑点花纹。画面轮廓外缘凿点极少，说明作画
认真娴熟。

侧面

27 狩猎·动物

汉
画面高50、宽48厘米
内蒙古自治区巴彦淖尔市乌拉特中旗温根镇几公海勒斯太采集

Hunting · Animal
Han Dynasty
Height: 50cm, Width: 48cm

凿刻制作。画面上方是两个骑马猎人，猎人持弓搭箭，正在寻找捕
猎对象，猎人所乘之马无鞍具，猎人下方有一人物和众多动物，动
物种类包括北山羊、马、狗、松鼠等。在猎人下方的一只北山羊已
被箭射中，背上刻有箭头。各种动物神态各异，造型准确生动，自
然流畅，充分展示了作画者娴熟的凿刻技巧和精湛的绘画才能。

28 女巫

汉
画面高35、宽26厘米
内蒙古自治区巴彦淖尔市乌拉特中旗温根镇几公海勒斯太采集

Witch

Han Dynasty
Height: 35cm, Width: 26cm

凿刻制作。女巫为正面像，戴头饰（或圆形法器）、系尾饰，双手平伸、腿叉开站立，乳房外露，一幅做法姿态。画面简单传神，动感十足。

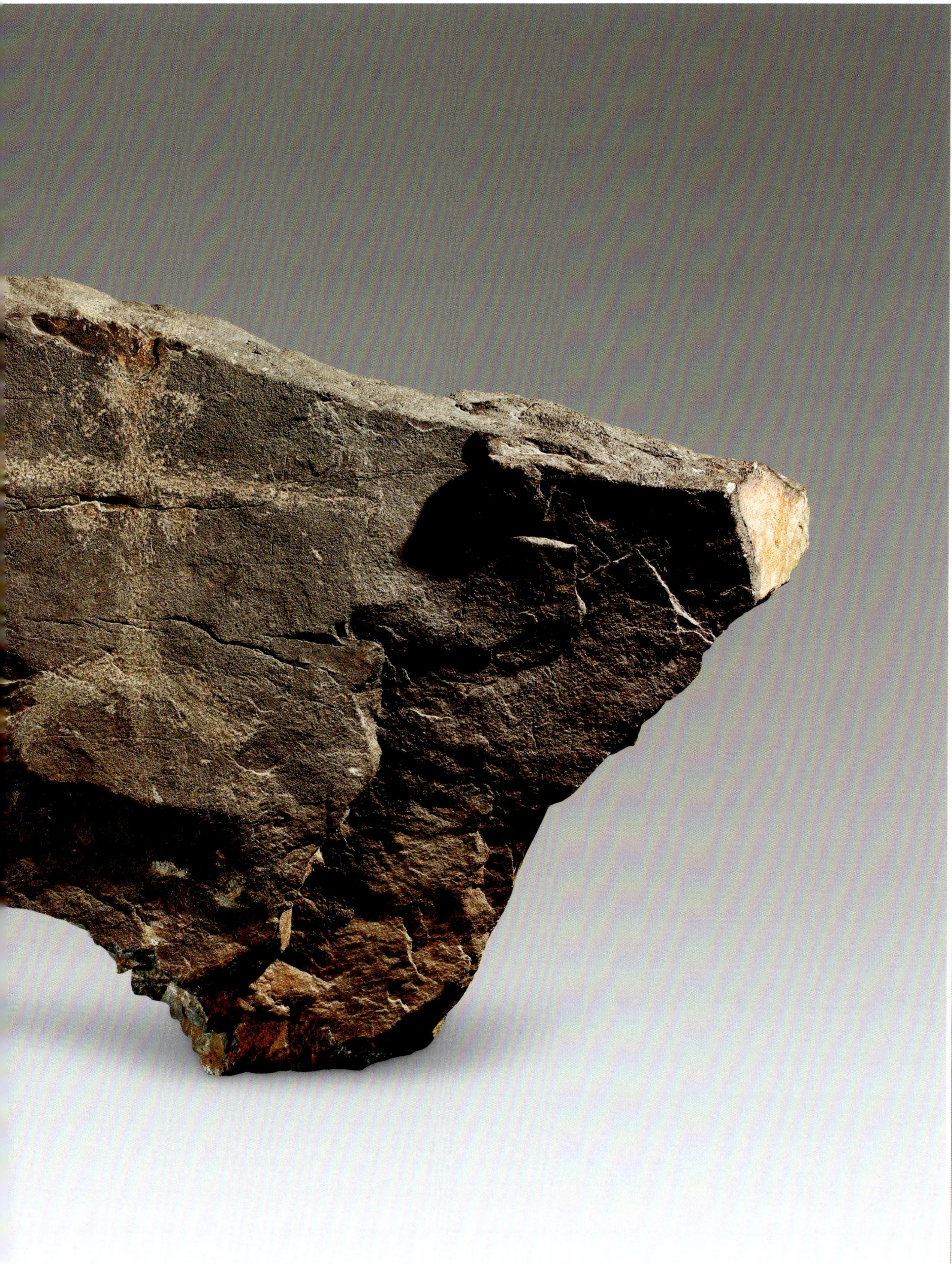

29 猎盘羊

汉
画面高36、宽36厘米
内蒙古自治区巴彦淖尔市乌拉特中旗温根镇几公海勒斯太采集

Argali-hunting
Han Dynasty
Height: 36cm, Width: 36cm

凿刻制作。画面为一个猎人和两只盘羊。猎人位于画面左下方，
系尾饰，引弓射中盘羊臀部；两只盘羊头向相反，羊角一前一后
盘旋成圆，极度夸张。画面一气呵成，极富感染力。

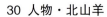

30 人物·北山羊

汉

画面高36、宽20厘米

内蒙古自治区巴彦淖尔市乌拉特中旗温根镇几公海勒斯太采集

Person · Capra ibex

Han Dynasty

Height: 36cm, Width: 20cm

凿刻制作。主体画面为一人立于北山羊背部位置，人物呈正面
像，系尾饰。北山羊侧身站立，羊角夸张，造型非常优美。

262

31 狼捕羊

汉

画面高29、宽36厘米

内蒙古自治区巴彦淖尔市乌拉特中旗温根镇几公海勒斯太采集

Capra ibex hunted by a wolf

Han Dynasty

Height: 29cm, Width: 36cm

凿刻制作。画面为一只狼正在追捕羊的场面，左侧一只北山羊呈奔跑状，后面狼紧追不舍，画面生动传神，反映了草原上弱肉强食的生态规律。作画趋于程式化。

32 人物·骑者·鹿·马·骆驼

汉—南北朝
画面高113、宽55厘米
内蒙古自治区巴彦淖尔市乌拉特中旗温根镇几公海勒斯太采集

Person · Rider · Deer · Horse · Camel
Han – Southern and Northern Dynasties
Height: 113cm, Width: 55cm

凿刻制作。主体画面从上到下分别刻着梅花鹿、骑者、马、人物、骆驼等。梅花鹿呈侧身奔跑状，鹿角夸张，十分华丽。骑者位于鹿下，无鞍具。骑者下为两匹马，侧身站立，再往下是两个人物和一峰骆驼，人物呈正面站立像，戴头饰（或发辫）、配腰刀。从作画风格和作画水平中不难看出，该岩画并非出自一人之手，其作画年代跨度较长，约为汉代至南北朝时期。

33 北山羊

西夏

画面高23、宽24厘米

内蒙古自治区巴彦淖尔市乌拉特中旗温根镇几公海勒斯太采集

Capra ibex

Western Xia

Height: 23cm, Width: 24cm

划刻制作。画面为一只昂首挺立的北山羊。作画用金属锐器划
出羊的轮廓，眼部以圆点刻出眼睛，为画面增添韵味。岩画风
格独特，整体造型优美，曲线流畅。

34 人面像

商周
画面高54、宽34厘米
内蒙古自治区阿拉善盟阿拉善左旗银根苏木查干哈达采集

Human Face
Shang and Zhou Periods
Height: 54cm, Width: 34cm

凿刻制作。画面为上下排列的三个人面形抽象图案（或人面具），
三个图案风格近似。以圆圈表示人脸，圈内象征性地刻有眼、鼻、
嘴（或牙齿）。图案很像一只从后向前透视的岩羊形状，以羊的两
只角表示眼睛，身体表示鼻子，四条腿表示嘴或牙齿。反映了所绘
图案与羊图腾有关。

35 人面像

商周
画面高36、宽38厘米
内蒙古自治区阿拉善盟阿拉善左旗银根苏木查干哈达采集

Human Face

Shang and Zhou Periods
Height: 36cm, Width: 38cm

凿刻制作。主体画面为一人面形图案，人面有眼、鼻、口、胡须，无耳。图像古朴抽象、庄严肃穆，作画精敲细琢。

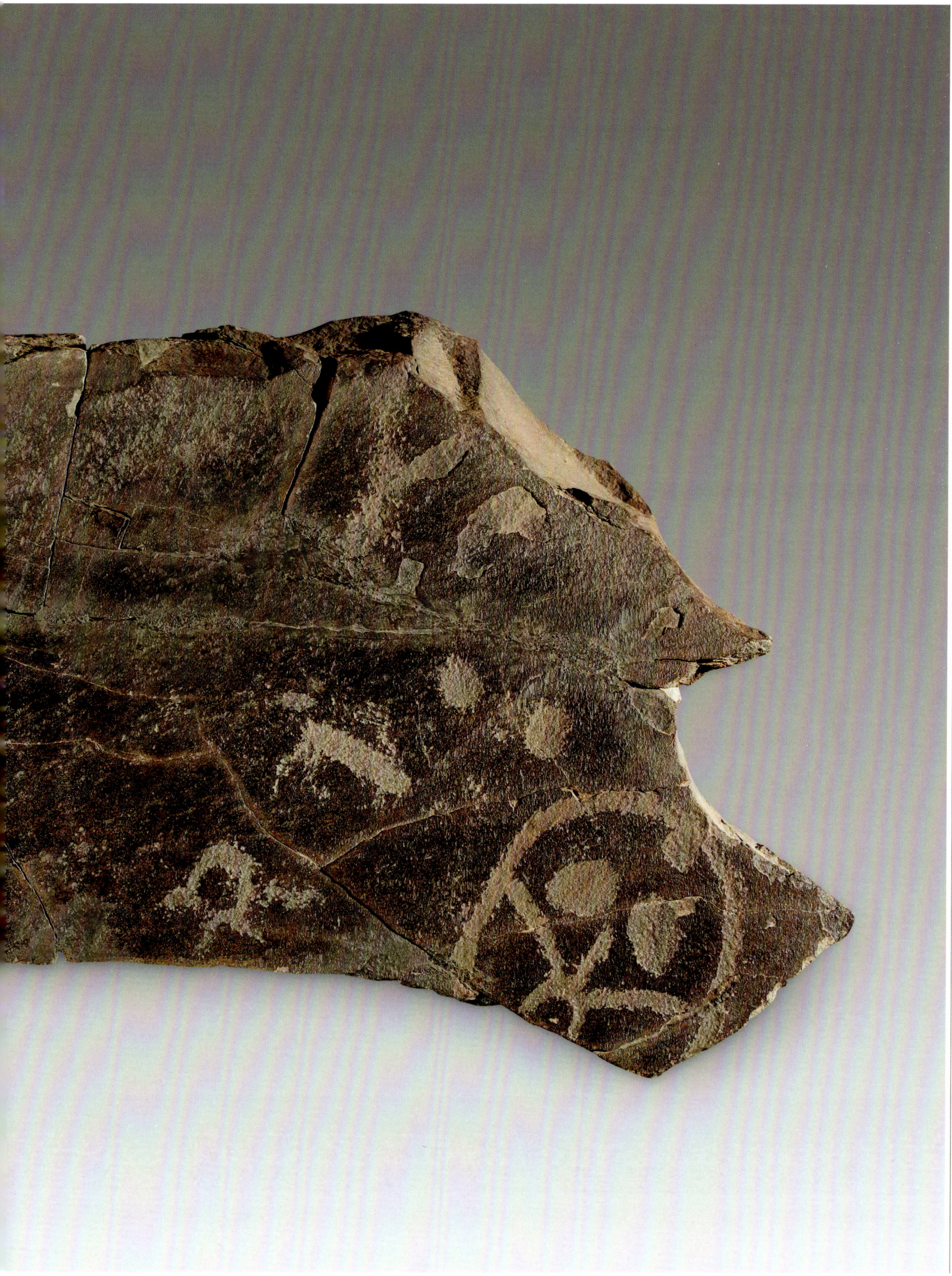

36 群舞图

商周
画面高40、宽27厘米
内蒙古自治区阿拉善盟阿拉善左旗腾格里额里斯苏木毕其格图山采集

Group dannce

Shang and Zhou Periods
Height: 40cm, Width: 27cm

凿刻制作。画面为上下成对排列的四个巫师形象，巫师均戴头饰（或系发辫），系尾饰，双手平伸，至肘部向下弯曲。其中左上方一人裸露乳房，成蹲坐姿势，为女性。另外三人呈骑马蹲裆式姿态，为典型的巫师作法动作。

37 太阳神·人·骑者

商周、南北朝
画面高31、宽48厘米
内蒙古自治区阿拉善盟阿拉善左旗银根苏木查干哈达采集

Apollo · Person · Rider

Shang and Zhou Periods, Southern and Northern Dynasties
Height: 31cm, Width: 48cm

凿刻制作。太阳神位于画面中央，上部刻一圆形，周围饰
光芒，以喻霞光四射，下面为一条竖线及一空心圆圈。整
个图案似一人形，采用的是拟人化的表现形式，这可能是
古人想象中的太阳神。太阳神的右侧为骑马者，备鞍具，
属早期马鞍的特征。太阳神属商周时代作品，人物和骑者
属南北朝时期作品。

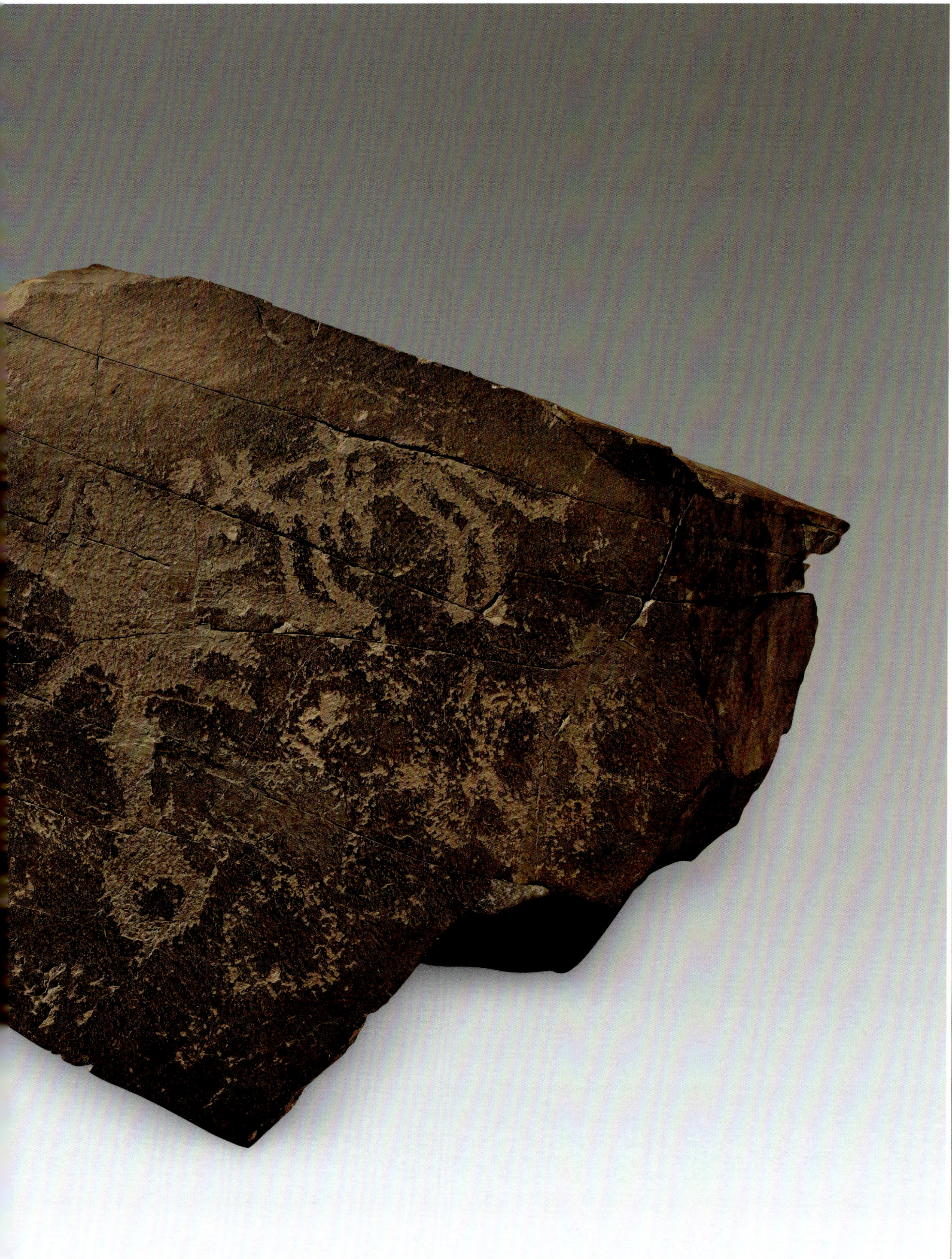

正面

38、39 围猎、马踏飞燕

春秋战国、汉
画面高90、宽60厘米；顶部画面高74、
宽31厘米
内蒙古自治区阿拉善盟阿拉善左旗腾
格里额里斯苏木希勒图山采集

**Group Hunting, Horse stepping
on flying swallow**
Spring and Autumn – Warring States
Period, Han Dynasty
Height: 90cm, Width: 60cm;
Height of the top: 74cm,
Width of the top: 31cm

凿刻制作。岩石的正面和顶面都刻有
画面，正面内容包括围猎、舞者、猎
马和各种动物。顶部画面刻有三四
马、一只燕（或鹰）和三只北山羊。
其中上方的一组画面最精彩，画面刻
绘出一匹奔腾的骏马和一只在马蹄下
飞翔的燕子，构成一幅精美的马踏飞
燕图。整幅岩画制作精致、构图完
美，是一幅非常难得的精品之作。围
猎图为春秋战国时期作品，马踏飞燕
为汉代作品。

顶部正面

40 骑者·动物

春秋战国、南北朝—唐
画面高58、宽50厘米
内蒙古自治区阿拉善盟阿拉善左旗腾格里额里斯苏木希勒图山采集

Rider · Animal

Spring and Autumn – Warring States Period,Southern and Northern Dynasties – Tang Dynasty
Height: 58cm, Width: 50cm

凿刻制作。画面内容包括骑者、北山羊、马、狼、虎等，岩画左上方两个骑者和一只北山羊颜色较浅，骑者所乘马都备有鞍具。右上方从上至下是北山羊、马和狼，北山羊和马的作画风格相同，都是以线条勾勒出身体轮廓。岩画的下方是两个骑者，其中，左侧骑马的人是后人补刻上去的，与马不是同一时代的作品，右下角是一只虎。岩画分为两个时期，其中颜色深的为春秋战国时期，较浅的为南北朝至唐代。

41 神话动物·羊群

战国
画面高52、宽31厘米
内蒙古自治区阿拉善盟阿拉善左旗腾格里额里斯苏木希勒图山采集

The mythical creature · sheep flock
Warring States Period
Height: 52cm, Width: 31cm

凿刻制作。画面内容是各种羊类和一个兽头羊身的神话动物。最上方是一排横向排列的盘羊，均侧身站立、头向一致、首尾相接。画面中部是三只北山羊和一只盘羊。再往下是两只羚羊一前一后横向排列，昂首伫立，目视远方。在两只羚羊中间有一只兽头羊身的神话动物，身体呈侧身站立，头为正面像，刻有三条腿。画面的最下方刻着一只飞奔的北山羊。

42 骑者·动物

战国
画面高34、宽47厘米
内蒙古自治区阿拉善盟阿拉善左旗腾格里额里斯苏木希勒图山采集

Rider · Animal
Warring States Period
Height: 34cm, Width: 47cm

凿刻制作。画面上方是横向排列的北山羊,头向一致朝右,首尾相
接,列队而行,羊的造型成侧身行走状,身体肥壮,颈上挺,吻前
伸,嘴张开作鸣叫状。画面构图精巧、动感十足。

43 骑者·犬·北山羊
战国—汉
画面高21、宽32厘米
内蒙古自治区阿拉善盟阿拉善左旗腾格里额里斯苏木希勒图山采集

Rider · Dog · Capra ibex
Warring States Period – Han Dynasty
Height: 21cm, Width: 32cm

凿刻制作。内容包括骑者、狗和北山羊。骑者位于左下方,在骑
者的上面和右侧是两只北山羊,北山羊的右上方是三只犬。

44 叉腰人

汉
画面高38、宽19厘米
内蒙古自治区阿拉善盟阿拉善左旗腾格里额里斯苏木毕其格图山采集

Akimbo person

Han Dynasty
Heigt: 38cm, Width: 19cm

凿刻制作。人物呈正面叉腰站立，以线条刻出人形，戴头饰，胸部刻
有两个圆点以示乳房。

45 人物·骑驼者·骆驼·马

汉

画面高56、宽50厘米

内蒙古自治区阿拉善盟阿拉善左旗腾格里额里斯苏木
毕其格图山采集

Person · Camel-rider · Camel · Horse
Han Dynasty
Height: 56cm, Width: 50cm

凿刻制作。画面上方是一个行走的人和一个骑驼者。
行者腰挎长刀，骑驼者一手持缰，骑坐于骆驼身上。
画面中部是两峰骆驼，由于石面残损，造成一骆驼画
面不全，另一峰骆驼通体凿刻，造型生动。画面下方
是两匹马，以线条刻出了马的身体轮廓。

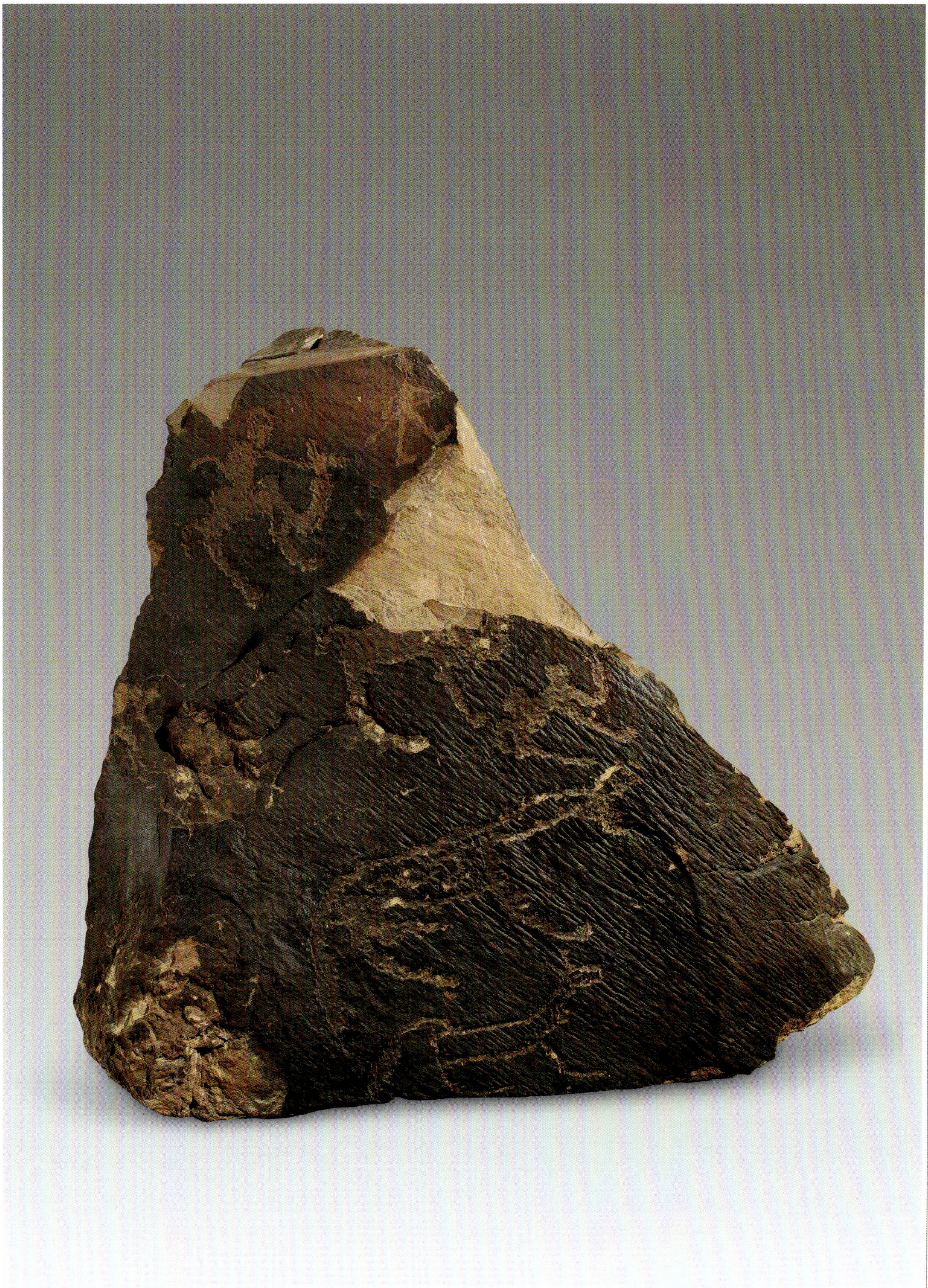

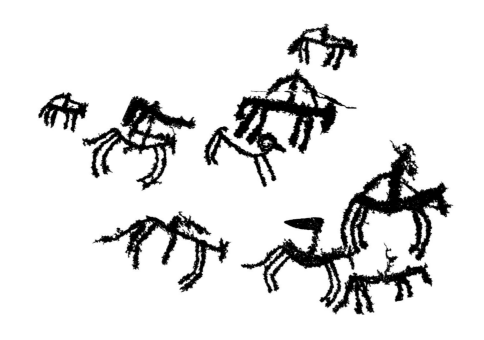

46 迁徙图

汉

画面高65、宽87厘米

内蒙古自治区阿拉善盟阿拉善左旗银根苏木查干哈达采集

Migration map

Han Dynasty

Height: 65cm, Width: 87cm

凿刻制作。画面内容有骑者和马、羊等家畜。均以线条表
现形象，个别骑者戴头饰。骑者与动物头向一致，结伴而
行，有迁徙之意。

47 骑马·骑驼·动物

西夏

画面高62、宽46厘米

内蒙古自治区 阿拉善盟阿拉善右旗孟根布拉格苏木曼德拉山采集

Horse-riding·Camel-riding·Animal

Western Xia

Height: 62cm, Width: 46cm

凿刻制作。画面内容为骑马者、骑驼者，羊、骆驼、狐狸、松鼠
等。骑驼者以线条凿刻出骑者和骆驼形象，骑者手持缰绳骑坐在
骆驼身上。骑驼者下方是骑马者，骑者所乘之马以线条刻出马的
轮廓，在轮廓内敲凿斑点以装饰。骑马者下方有一大一小两峰骆
驼，大骆驼侧身站立，小骆驼正在大骆驼肚下吮奶。反映了草原
上祥和安宁的放牧场景。

48 牦牛

西夏
画面高25、宽27厘米
内蒙古自治区阿拉善盟阿拉善右旗孟根布拉格苏木曼德拉山采集

Yak

Western Xia
Height: 25cm, Width: 27cm

凿刻制作。牦牛造型生动具象，肌肉、关节、皮毛都表现得非常
细腻，牛角夸张，尾巴高高扬起，极富动感。

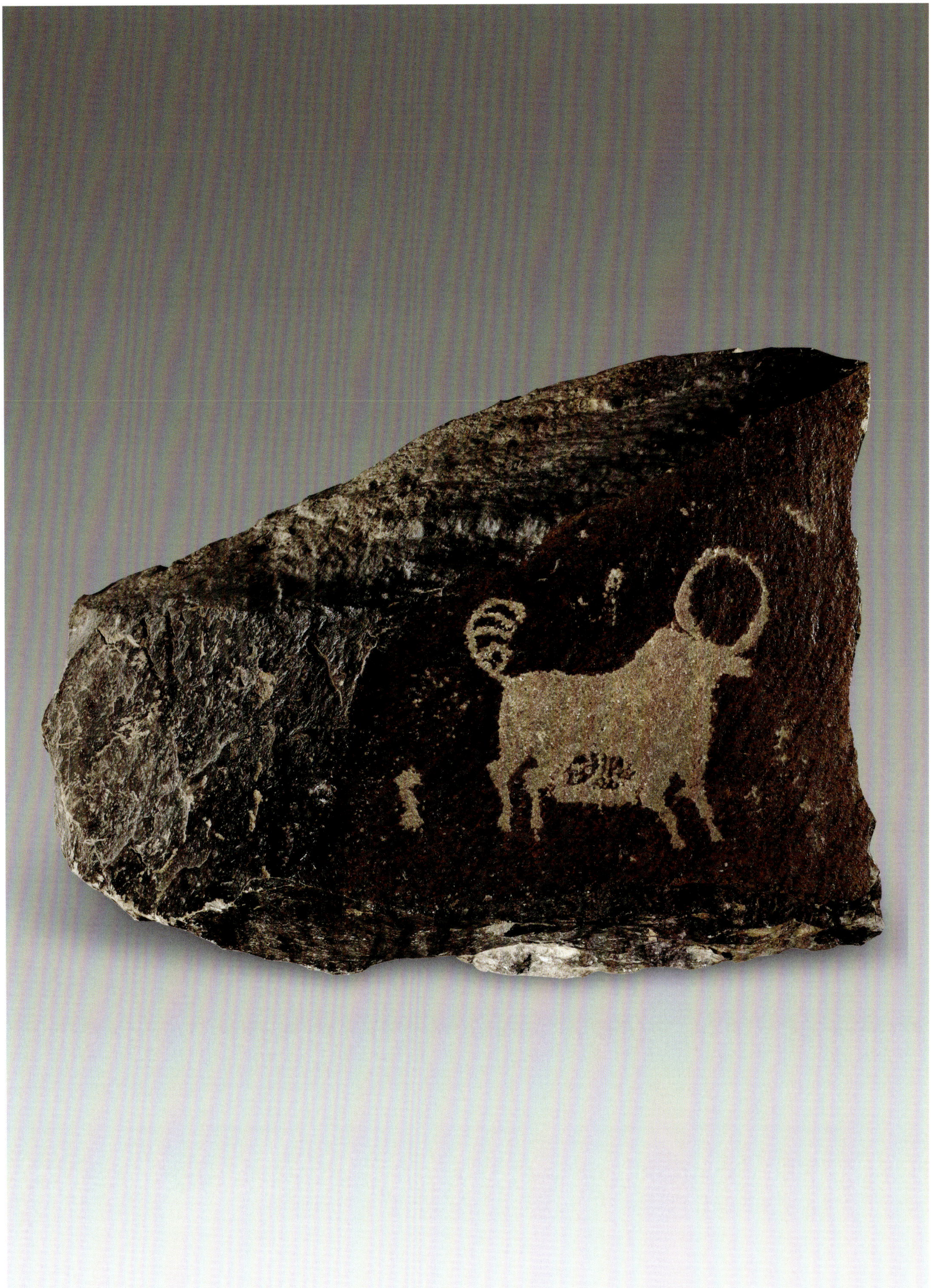

49 人物·马·虎

西夏
画面高20、宽62厘米
内蒙古自治区阿拉善盟阿拉善右旗孟根布拉格苏木曼德拉山采集

Person · Horse · Tiger
Western Xia
Height: 20cm, Width: 62cm

凿刻制作。人物位于画面中央，戴头饰、穿长袍、双手上举，呈
祈祷状，马立于画面左侧，配马鞍。虎位于画面右侧，造型生
动、气宇轩昂、威风凛凛。整幅画面造型准确、凿刻精致。

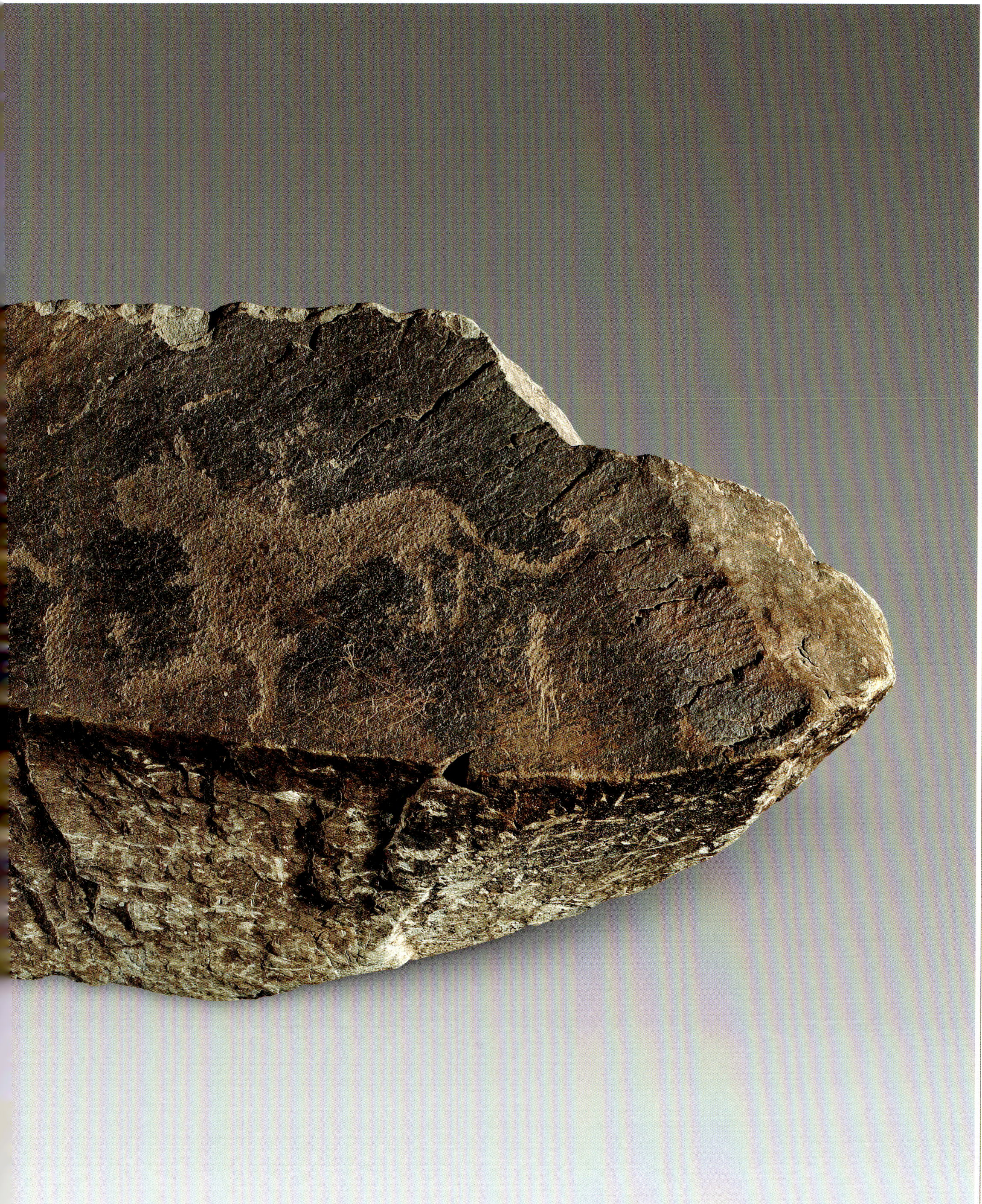

50 古藏文

明

画面高23、宽36厘米

内蒙古自治区阿拉善盟阿拉善右旗孟根布拉格苏木曼德拉山采集

The ancient Tibetan

Ming Dynasty

Height: 23cm, Width: 36cm

凿刻制作。文字系古藏文，意为"敬礼佛、敬礼大菩提、敬礼大菩提"，为佛教用语。画面上方是一只北山羊，图形简单，造型趋于程式化。

51 北山羊·犬·藏文

清
画面高81、宽50厘米
内蒙古自治区阿拉善盟阿拉善左旗腾格里额里斯苏木毕其格图山采集

Capra ibex · Dog · Tibetan
Qing Dynasty
Height: 81cm, Width: 50cm

凿刻制作。北山羊位于画面上方，呈侧身站立，昂首挺颈，吻前伸，张嘴鸣叫。北山羊下边是一只犬，以线条勾勒出身体轮廓，造型活泼洒脱，线条流畅自然，动感十足。画面下方为两个藏文，属佛教用语，与藏传佛教有关。

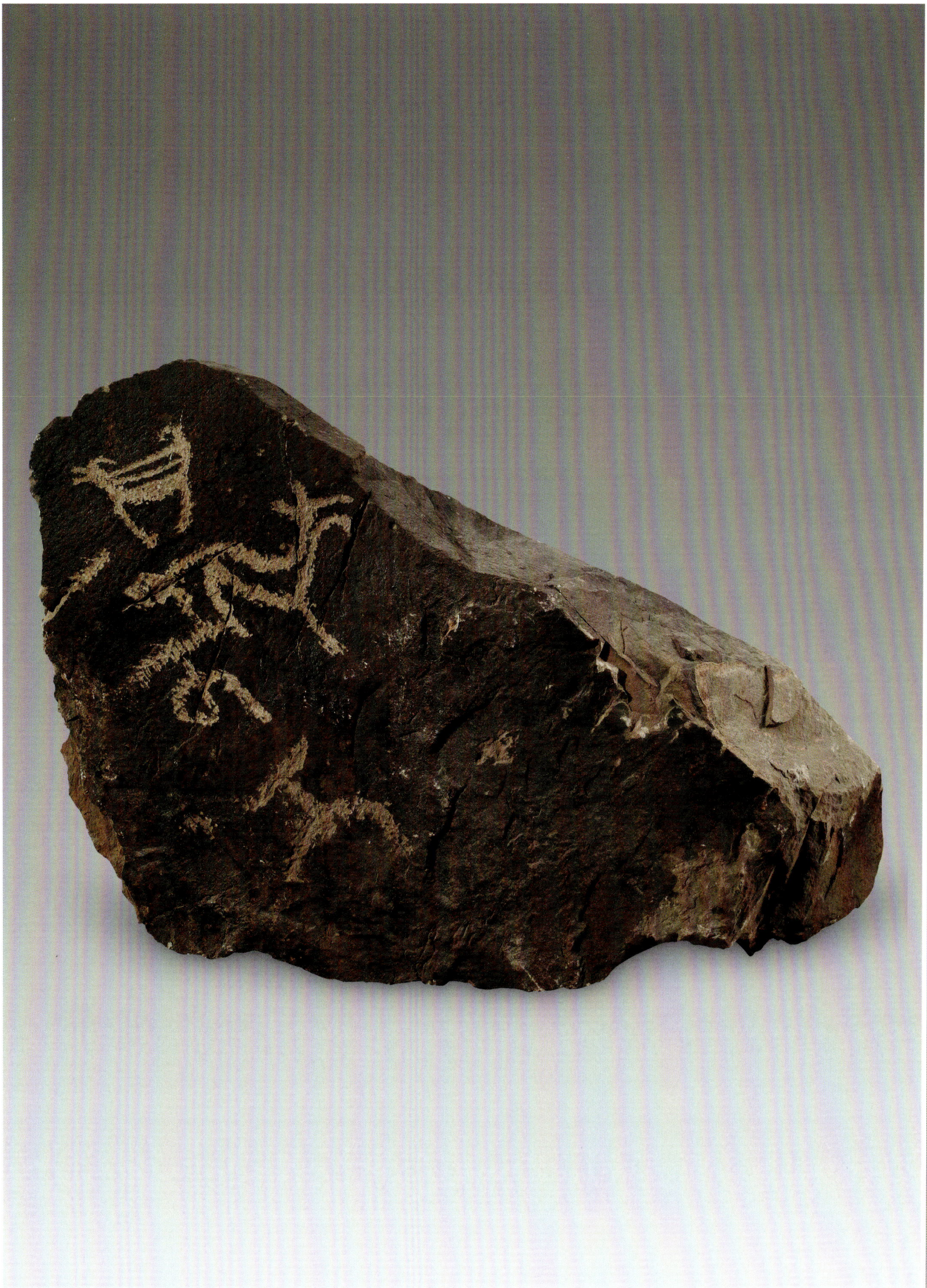

后 记

几经努力，《内蒙古包头博物馆馆藏文物集萃》终于问世，本书收录了包头博物馆最具特色、最能代表包头地域文化的文物精品，以彰显包头深厚的文化底蕴和博大精深的文化内涵。

在本书编辑过程中，得到了中共包头市委常委、宣传部孙红梅部长的关心支持，亲自作序；内蒙古博物院塔拉院长也欣然作序，并给予高度评价；包头市文化局洪涛局长多次嘉勉；内蒙古博物院郑承燕女士为本书做英文翻译。能得到众多领导、专家和同行的关心支持，我们非常感动。在此，特向他们表达谢意！亦对关心、支持本书出版的社会各界朋友表示衷心的感谢！向为本书出版付出艰辛努力的所有人士表示深深的敬意！

本书文物鉴选与器物描述由姜涛、李彩霞、王磊义、杨君、赵小平、龚鹏等同仁承担。由于编者水平有限，不足与偏颇在所难免，敬请指正。

编　者
2012年9月

POSTSCRIPT

We finally publish *Selection of Baotou Museum Collection* after year's effort. Editing the catalogue of cultural relics with outstanding characteristics and representing the regional culture, we are aimed to present the deep cultural information and profound cultural connotation of Baotou City.

We express sincerely thanks to many friends as followings: Sun Hongmei, standing committee and director of Propaganda Department of Baotou Municipal Committee of the CPC, who concerns the publishing of the catalogue and endows the preface I by herself; Ta La, director of Inner Mongolia Museum, who writes the preface II in person and highly values this catalogue; Hong Tao, director of Baotou Cultural Administration, who praised and encouraged us many times; Zheng Chengyan, who translates the catalogue. We really appreciate the support from the friends in social circles and the colleagues who pay great efforts to the publishing of it.

Our fellow colleagues Jiang Tao, Li Caixia, Wang Leiyi, Yang Jun, Zhao Xiaoping and Gong Peng select and describe the cultural relics in the catalogue. Due to the limited level of editors, please don't hesitate to correct us if any deficiencies and biases occur.

The editors
September, 2012

责任印制：陈　杰

责任编辑：李　飏

图书在版编目（ＣＩＰ）数据

　内蒙古包头博物馆馆藏文物集萃 ／ 内蒙古包头博物
馆编．－－北京 ：文物出版社，2012.10
　　ISBN 978－7－5010－3546－5

　Ⅰ．①内… Ⅱ．①内… Ⅲ．①博物馆－历史文物－包
头市 Ⅳ．①K872.263

　中国版本图书馆CIP数据核字(2012)第213359号

内蒙古包头博物馆馆藏文物集萃

编　　者　内蒙古包头博物馆
_____

出版发行　文物出版社
社　　址　北京市东直门内北小街2号楼
网　　址　www.wenwu.com
邮　　箱　web@wenwu.com
制　　版　北京图文天地制版印刷有限公司
印　　刷　北京图文天地制版印刷有限公司
经　　销　新华书店
开　　本　889×1194　1/16
印　　张　19
版　　次　2012年10月第1版
印　　次　2012年10月第1次印刷
书　　号　ISBN 978－7－5010－3546－5
定　　价　380.00元